ENJOY LIFE
NOW

Biblical Secrets To Enjoying Life
On A Daily Basis

By Beverly Angel

*Spirit***Library**
PUBLICATIONS

ENJOY LIFE
NOW

Biblical Secrets To Enjoying Life
On A Daily Basis

Unless otherwise stated, all scripture quotations are taken
from the King James Version of the Bible.

ISBN 978-0-955 8116-9-2

Copyright 2010 by Beverly Angel

Published by Spirit Library Publications

Contents

1 CHAPTER ONE *7*
You Can Enjoy Life, Right Now!

2 CHAPTER TWO *25*
What Is Joy Anyway

3 CHAPTER THREE *51*
The Force Of Peace

4 CHAPTER FOUR *73*
Take A Hold Of Longsuffering

5 CHAPTER FIVE *93*
Be Kind

6 CHAPTER SIX *99*
Goodness

7 CHAPTER SEVEN *115*
Be Filled With Faithfulness

8 CHAPTER EIGHT *127*
Joy And Gentleness

9 CHAPTER NINE *139*
Have Temperance

CHAPTER ONE

You Can Enjoy Life, Right Now!

I have had opportunities and still do, of meeting Presidents, Prime Ministers, wealthy people and celebrities around the world. I travel the world often, own and run businesses from publishing to luxury hotels. I have been to some of the best holiday resorts and lived in some of the highest rated hotels in the world, drove the best cars, seen the things few have had the chance to see all their lives, been acquainted to wealthy personalities in the world BUT all this does not make one enjoy life on a daily basis. That I have come to know is a fact!

Notice that there are many wealthy and celebrated people I know personally, who have too many expensive cars but are going nowhere, too many mansions with one too many therapeutic beds but finding no sleep and two many pairs of shoes but leading them nowhere.

Joy is not about the material things it is about something way deeper than material things or even happiness. Here I am not saying material things will not help you. No don't get me wrong, I am not saying that at all. What I am here to say is you can enjoy your life right NOW, regardless of what you have or do not have! It is possible. It can be done.

If you do not learn to enjoy life now even material things will mean nothing when they come your way.

Make The Choice To Create Joy

There are three kinds of people in the world. Those who make things happen, those who watch things happen and those who ask what happenned? With regards to joy, you should make it happen regardless of the circumstances you face. In this life, with all the problems and hardships that people may face, some can decide to pursue joy yet others can decide to create joy. You can decide to move in joy today. You can live a stress free life. You can choose to bring out the joy in you and let the world know you as a person who is not moved by any circumstance. You can be filled with joy unspeakable. Yes, today as a believer in Christ. It can be done!

It's Not About What You Have

Enjoying life is not about what you have, it is a choice. It is a choice to follow principles that will bring joy everywhere you are, at any stage of life and at any time. It is a choice to adopt steps that will wipe away a frown and bring a smile twenty four hours a day and seven days a week. This life of joy is possible. It can be achieved. I have done it and I know beyond depth and beyond height that the life of joy can be yours at whatever stage you are in life. You can enjoy life, right here and now!

This is the life created for the believer. It is a life of continuous joy, a life with no side effects. It is a life of an over-comer. This is the life that impregnated Apostle Paul that with all the pain the world was pushing his direction he was still filled with joy that he uttered;

"...none of these things move me..."

Acts 20:24

Now, I want to stress before I go any further that it does not matter where you are in your life right now. It matters nothing whether yesterday is a bad memory, today is a challenge or tomorrow is simply a mystery filled with painful hours and minutes to you. If you learn to enjoy right now, today, even yesterday will become a memory of happiness as you turn bad memories into learning curves, today will be a miracle and every tomorrow will automatically change into an opportunity for more smiles and no worries. God has made it possible to the extent that He has created a problem free zone for those who believe Him.

He says,

"Do not worry what you shall eat, drink or wear...tomorrow will worry for itself..."

Matthew 6:31, 34

These are His own words, nothing of mine. God Himself says there is a life where worry cannot exist, where stress is nonexistent and where depression cannot find you. In the above verse, He proves this life is possible hence the directive.

"...Do not worry..."

You are not even allowed to worry. God does not want you to worry. He knows a secret deeper than happiness. Deeper than all the smiles the world can offer. He knows and he is the giver of joy and this joy is for you today.

See, the absence of worry equals the presence of peace, joy and hope. Notice again the scripture above. God is not saying worrying is bad. No he is not saying that at all. What He is saying is some may worry but not you who are called by his name. Some may fret and worry but as for you, God wants you to be worry repellent. Worry proof. God says worrying about tomorrow is alright as long as IT IS NOT YOU doing the worrying. God Himself says Tomorrow will do the worrying for you NOT YOU. Your duty is to enjoy life and the duty of tomorrow is to worry about itself.

Living An Expected Life

I have been to holiday resorts that promised happiness and joy and have attended conferences on how to enjoy life. They told me things I swallowed hook, line, sinker, the fisherman, his boots and the stool he sat on, but all was void. There was a lot of hot air and nothing that helped until God awakened me to principles that were in the word that will without fail promote joy unspeakable. These principles were there since the beginning of time but I had not gotten myself to a level where I believed in what I had confessed I believed.

I took those principles and my husband and I followed them without fail. We rigorously set out to prove God and yes He is faithful. His principles worked in our lives and still work today. After we realised these things we introduced a program where we take couples quarterly on what we have coined 'the couples retreat' held in a certain castle on a mountain where we teach these principles in different ways and this has proven to be a hit with many couples.   We have since extended this to include singles, old and young people and many people's lives have been changed. It is real; life can be full of joy today!

With God it is possible. This joy I am leading you to see is the joy that has a different focus. It looks to the Lord not just to perform but to destroy the seen by what is unseen to the mind. I shall explain this later. However before that just look at how the word of God puts it.

"Rejoice in the Lord always [delight, gladden

yourselves in Him]; again I say, Rejoice!"

Philippians 4:4

This is a command to rejoice. How many times a week should I do this? Always!

If you do not choose to learn the principles that bring joy to your life, life for you will be filled with incidentals; things you feel you have to do but in fact of little or no benefit to you. I have been there, done that, bought the t-shirt and eventually burnt it. There is a reason why God would give us the mandate to rejoice in a way that seems as if I am ordering it to happen. It's in a commanding tone.

One just needs to learn how to live this life free of fear and worry, kick back, relax, be at ease and enjoy life right now!

The Character of Possibility Thinking

"...As a man thinketh in his heart so is he..."

Proverbs 23:7

If you can think it up, you can bring it down. If you think these principles being God revealed are difficult just because you see God as an angry autocrat sitting in heaven with a hundred pound hammer in His hand, waiting to pounce on any of his children and kill if they misbehave then you will get nothing. However if you think of God as a loving father who wants to maximise your life by putting joy in you then you will receive this revelation.

I say this because many who hear that there is a life God desires everyone to have, they cringe, thinking if its God who requires it from them then it is difficult to achieve when in actual fact it is the easiest of all. You see, there is a character that God desires every believer to possess and in that character lies the secret to enjoying life. This character list is in itself a container of attitude that if adopted, will lead into a life full of joy and no worries.

Apostle Paul refers to it in a form of an 'orchard'. This 'orchard' can catapult a believer into a level where there is no pain and into a land of joy, and here I mean absolute joy which can be achieved today as you decide to take time to follow these principles and put them to work yourself. If you think it's impossible to do then you have already locked your spirit from what will bring joy to you regardless of the difficulties you may be faced with.

Yes, this joy can be achieved. We, as the children of God are meant to have this joy and are meant to be so contagious with this joy that there is no way we cannot infect our world with it. This is what this whole book is about; having joy unspeakable and being contagious like a rash and being able to spread it around. I have witnessed several times in our church meetings people laughing from deep inside after being filled with joy unspeakable. This laughter anointing is so contagious that we often times have half the church laughing from deep inside their spirit and spontaneous and extreme miracles take place. It is just like medicine as the Bible rightly puts it;

"...a merry heart doeth good like a medicine..."

Proverbs 17:22

The Secret

The biggest secret about the principles to joy is that they control your spirit, soul and body. They do not only control your spirit. They also control your soul and your body so they will definitely bring about an overhaul of your life. This is proven and you ought to let every fibre of your being, every pore of your body and every cell of your blood soak into these principles.

It is a surprise that all these principles are crammed into one verse and are very publicly available but we have not read between the lines and learnt what they mean and how to employ them. A few people that have tried them have applied them but in a wrong way due to lack of revelation of what they really are. I admit that at face value you might think they are easy to understand but there is reason why the word says:

"...rightly dividing the word of truth..."

2 Timothy 2:15

The word needs revelation for it is a field of

goodies hidden from those who have not dedicated themselves to these things. The word needs those with eyes that are anointed with eye salve. These principles here might really look easy but they carry a deeper meaning which the Lord revealed to me.

Notice what Apostle Paul said in reference to this secret to joy in the book of Galatians chapter 5:22-23:

But the fruit of the Spirit is love, joy, peace, longsuffering, kindness, goodness, faithfulness, gentleness, self-control.

Love And Its Parts

There is a revelation you need to catch before I explain this fruit of the Spirit. God told me the fruit of the Spirit is actually one. Stay with the word here and it will fix your problems in understanding this. No wonder the Bible puts it as fruit and not fruits as for plural.

Galatians says fruit but lists nine. Here there is a way to understand this which is very simple. Love is the overall fruit but the other eight are really parts of the fruit just as we have fruits with the outer covering, the flesh and the seed. The seed here will be part of the fruit but not the fruit.

The outer shell or skin and the flesh of the fruit are simply parts but not the fruit. Love also is the fruit but joy, peace, longsuffering, kindness, goodness, faithfulness, gentleness, self-control are simply parts of the fruit. I want you to stay with this thought for a minute and see how it will explain the principle of joy. See we need to build a foundation before building a building so if I move quickly to the principles before laying the foundation, the building will not stand so stay with this thought for a moment.

The Proof For Love And Its Parts

I have said love is the only fruit and all the others are parts of the fruit. Here is why. We know the Lord Jesus gave love as the only commandment for the believer and also understand that the Lord says the truth should be established in the presence of two or three witnesses so we need to look deep into the word to see how this works. Look at Galatians again;

But the fruit of the Spirit is love, joy, peace, longsuffering, kindness, goodness, faithfulness, gentleness, self-control. Compare this to **1 Corinthians 13: 4-8**

Love suffers long and is kind; love does not envy; love does not parade itself, is not puffed up; does not behave rudely, does not seek its own, is not provoked, thinks no evil; does not rejoice in iniquity, but rejoices in the truth; bears all things, believes all things, hopes all things, endures all things. Love never fails.

The fruit of the Spirit in Galatians 5:22-23 is actually listed under love here in the book of 1

Corinthians 13:4-8. If closely analysed these two scriptures say 'Love suffers long'. What is that? That sounds like longsuffering. 'And is kind', what is that? That is kindness. **'Love does not envy, love does not parade itself it's not puffed up'.** What is that? Peace. **'Love does not behave rudely, does not seek its own, and is not provoked',** what is that? Gentleness. **'Thinks no evil'**, that is Goodness, **'Does not rejoice in iniquity but rejoices in the truth',** what is that? Joy. **'Bears all things, believes all things, hopes all things',** what is that? That is faithfulness.

So I will explain love first before I break it down to the components of it and that will open up our understanding to what it really is and how to exercise the fruit of the Spirit in order to have joy in abundance. This joy is unsurpassed. It is incomparable. I know it. I have it on a daily basis regardless of what the devil throws at me.

Love

In explaining what love according to God is we need to look at the word 'love' itself. It has distinct differences that I want to touch on a little. The Greek word agape is often translated "love" in the New Testament. How is "agape love" different from other types of love? The essence of agape love is self-sacrifice. Unlike our English word "love," agape is not used in the Bible to refer to romantic or sexual love. Nor does it refer to close friendship or brotherly love, for which the

Greek word philia is used. Nor does agape mean charity, a term which the King James translators carried over from the Latin. Agape love is unique and is distinguished by its nature and character.

Agape is love which is of and from God, whose very nature is love itself. The Apostle John affirms this in 1 John 4:8, "God is love." God does not merely love; He is love itself. Everything God does flows from His unending love. Realise that the love that is spoken about here is not the 'fuzzy feeling' that we often portray. The God kind of love is His nature and the expression of His being. He loves us even when we highly do not deserve to be loved by Him. Why does God do this? It's His nature to do so that's why. Christ died for us and this is an ultimate display of God's love toward us. We did nothing to deserve it. The Bible says,

 "...but God commends His love toward us in that while we were yet sinners Christ died for us"

Romans 5:8

Agape love never does anything to merit His love. This love is independent of what happens. It's not influenced by happenings just like joy unspeakable as said before.

How To Adopt It

 The God kind of love does not come naturally as people are born. Because of our fallen nature, we are incapable of producing such a love. Only born again Christians have this love as the Bible says;

"The love of God is shed in our hearts by the Holy Spirit"

Romans 5:5

As believers according to the word of God, His love is placed in our hearts when we accept the Lord Jesus as our personal Saviour. That means we have this love already even when we don't feel like it. What we might fail to have is the acting upon it and we ought to act upon this love. If your spouse is acting like your arch enemy exercise love by using the parts of love that make it a whole fruit. When your boss seems as if he resides in the uttermost pits of hell, still love him. When your mother-in-law is acting as if she is the devil incarnate, still love her. Love never goes wrong. Fruits of the spirit only work if love works. You cannot have joy in abundance and enjoy life if you do not exercise the love that God has shed abroad in your heart. In a way, joy is simply part of the fruit called love.

Love And Joy In The Face Of Persecution

See, love is a motivator and faith an activator. When love controls you, it makes you a master in life. It makes you a conqueror. Nothing moves you. Nothing gets you perturbed. Nothing and absolutely nothing gets you disturbed. Love is a master in life.

We have faced a lot of people saying all sorts of

things about us, persecuting us for no reason. Some misconstrue the truth and some don't even want to hear the truth. We have seen many oppose the work that God gave us to do with ill gotten information. Instead of coming forward and asking us about these same matters, they decide from their sources' information yet the Bible says only a fool decides a matter after hearing one side. We did not try to explain ourselves for enemies never want to hear the truth. They don't need the truth, it does not settle well with them. They take pleasure in your destruction.

I remember a time when it used to hurt knowing what lies people were spreading about us. I could not understand why the people that we helped the most were the very ones who would turn around and stab us in the back. THEN and this is a big then, the Lord taught us the principles that bring joy in any circumstance and ever since it has been a roller coaster of happiness in our lives. I cannot think of anything that will let me lose my joy. It cannot happen. The love of God in me contains full joy as the word says:

"The joy of the Lord is my strength In the Midst of my Enemies"

Nehemiah 8:10

Now, I cannot think of any person I hate. There is none. I can safely say I have no enemies. This might be difficult for some because they might feel that it's impossible not to have enemies. But that is not what I am saying. What I am saying is I have people that hate me with all their heart.

There are some that will continue to hate me with all their heart but I don't hate them back. In fact, I love them. By this statement of reality you can safely see that love is more than a fuzzy feeling. Love is not just a feeling you feel. It is a decision to follow parts that add up to love.

Many who will read the fruit of the Spirit in the Bible will think they already know what love is all about and there is no amount of convincing that can show them that they do not have any idea what love is. However in the next chapters you will be covered by an anointing of revelation that will open up the reality of these principles to the extent where you will say, 'I really did not understand love, now I know the fullness of it and what it carries to make it a fruit'.

Love has parts just like a fruit has parts like skin, seeds and flesh, and these have to be put into practice and explained for them to start working in you.

You can have joy, real joy. There are a lot of problems around that it begs no argument that there is a need to have something that makes one soar above problems and circumstances, something that neither relies on feelings nor circumstances.

An Experience In Life

I remember my husband's mentor telling us a story about an incident that happened to him way back. He had heard that there was a man calling him all sorts of names. This man had said among other things that he was a false prophet. One night he could not sleep thinking how this man could be so cold to lie and call him a false prophet when there was enough evidence to the contrary. Because of this he could not sleep a wink. Early in the morning the next day, he called his friend set to go and confront this man. They arrived at the man's house very early in the morning and knocked on his door. It took a while for him to open the door and when he did, he showed he was just waking up from a deep sleep.

The man had been sleeping soundly yet my husband's mentor had not slept at all thinking about this man. Immediately as he thought of this injustice, God spoke to him and said, "You see this man was sleeping after all the evil he did to you and you could not find any sleep because of him". When he heard that he turned around and left and vowed that he would not let anything move him except love. He said if the one who is doing me wrong can find sleep yet he is being used of the devil, I will find better sleep because I am used by God. After all the word says:

"...He will give his beloved sleep..."

Psalm 127:2

He got a hold of the revelation of the components of the love fruit to the extent that he is now one of the most sought after prophets in the world because of the profound integrity that stems from understanding how the components of love work. Joy is a component of the fruit of love which works by being part of all the other components and with one component missing a person can never have full joy.

See, to have joy, one must get that understanding that there are components to be followed and that revelation will without fail make you enjoy life now!

The Three Groups

What makes this revelation of superior power to other subjects devoted to joy is that this is God given and also that this covers the whole person, spirit, soul and body. At the same time the components of love as the fruit of the Spirit are also in groups by themselves.

These groups are in connection with the spirit, soul and body. This fruit controls your spirit, controls your soul and controls your body. As you may know, we are spirit beings, who possess a soul and live in a body. If you look again at Galatians 5:22-23, you will notice that the first two parts of love as the fruit of the Spirit joy and peace are always the basic control of our spirit man. If your spirit man is right with God, you will always sense love which promotes joy and peace over your spirit. However these need to be explained, they do not just stand as joy and peace. There is a deeper revelation which I will explain here that will shock you and propel you into the land of joy.

After that there are three called longsuffering,

kindness and goodness which have everything to do with the fruit of the Spirit growing forth and controlling your soul. Your soul consists of mind, will and emotions, so longsuffering, kindness and goodness control your mind, will and emotions. They control your soul. The last three faithfulness, gentleness and self-control speak of control that rises from your spirit through the Holy Spirit upon your body and master it into submission to the will of the Spirit and in turn, the control of all these three areas by the Spirit bring joy.

These principles will have your spirit, your soul and your body subordinate to the spiritual influences of the Holy Spirit.

Prepare For Joy

We will touch these groups in a way God has taught me and move you into a level where you will not only understand joy in a different way but where joy in you does not cease. A life that is not dependent upon what happens in order to rejoice. A life loaded with joy unspeakable. A life of champions and winners. A life reserved for the best.

Now kick back, relax, be at ease and prepare to enjoy life right now!

CHAPTER TWO

What Is Joy Anyway?

The Biblical Greek term from Paul's spiritual orchard in Galatians is chara which means joy, cheer or celebration. Joy is intense, ecstatic and exultant pleasure.

This kind of Joy runs deeper than mere pleasure. It goes deeper than any kind of happiness. This joy runs deep into the core of us, and radiates throughout the spirit and shows on the body. It is the response of the human Spirit to God Himself so it is supreme, and also overpoweringly strong. The devil and his gang cannot stand a believer with such joy. They quiver at the mere sight of a believer with this intense, ecstatic and exultant pleasure.

Joy Versus Happiness

Joy has nothing to do with happiness. Pure joy cannot be mistaken for happiness. "Happiness" comes from the word "happen."

Happiness, therefore, is based on what is happening. If something good is happening, then you are happy. If feelings allow it then you become happy. However, God says that pure joy occurs even in the midst of trials even when there is no money, when the worst is happening, when the cat is running with the dog, when the wife is with the gardener and the husband is with the maid. It does not matter what is happening, joy will find a way to have a great day.

Joy breaks out even when the situation does not allow.

Notice real joy here in **Habakkuk 3:17:**

"Though the fig tree does not bud and there are no grapes on the vines, though the olive crop fails and the fields produce no food, though there are no sheep in the pen and no cattle in the stalls, YET..."

How can Habakkuk say "YET...", when he had nothing to show for anything? He was in serious hardships. Things were out of hand. Hunger was all over, persecution was all over. In fact in the first part of the first chapter, the Prophet sees the injustice among his people and asks God why he is not taking action;

"...how long will I cry, and you will not hear? I cry out to you 'Violence!' and will you not save?"

Habakkuk 1:2

The Prophet here was in a dilemma. He was in serious problems yet the word YET exists in his mouth. See what he said;

He says, **"Yet I will REJOICE IN THE LORD, I will be JOYFUL IN GOD MY SAVIOR" (Chapter 3:18).**

Notice, he was not going to surrender to his problems. He was going to do something about his problems. He had chosen to remain joyous. Happiness could not be there because it relies on the happenings and here the happenings were bad. Notice it was not only about the drought in the fields or the sheep not being in the pen or about cattle missing from the stalls. It was something of great pain.

The joy of Habakkuk can be yours

The only plain time reference in this prophecy is chapter 1:6, where the Lord says, "I am raising up the Chaldeans". Actually, the Chaldeans were a tribe of Semites from southern Babylonia, who became rulers of the Neo-Babylonian Empire.

Therefore, the prophet goes to God and asks some difficult questions, and he receives some answers which greatly puzzle him. Nevertheless, through it all, whether he understands or not, his faith in God never wavers because there was joy inside of him. Habakkuk's situation was deeply troubling. How could God permit so much suffering and death? How could God punish His own people, even though they had sinned, by using a nation that was even more wicked than they? How can a righteous God use the wicked Chaldeans to punish

His people, which, in spite of its sins, is still more righteous than the country God is raising against it? This was a situation where God seemed to be supporting Habakkuk's enemies! Violence and law-breaking abounded, and the wicked seemed at least superficially, to triumph. According to all that Habakkuk knew about God's holiness and covenant, Deuteronomy chapters 26-33, on which Habakkuk seemed dependent, Yahweh should have arisen to correct the situation, particularly in response to believing prayer for change by him. Such correction had not been forthcoming, and the prayers of the righteous seemed to be ignored.

This is a time when you think anyone should give up, BUT Habakkuk says:

"...YET..."

He is going to REJOICE because,

"The Sovereign Lord is my strength; he makes my feet like the feet of a deer, he enables me to go on the heights" (chapter 3:19).

You see, Habakkuk had no intention of staying defeated. He may look defeated, but he is not going to stay defeated. The difference between the person who is defeated and the person who is victorious is their JOY.

An attitude of joy will put you over in life. It will make you a master in life. This is the kind of attitude that this prophet had. Even though nothing good was happening in his life; no fruit, no crops, no sheep, no cattle, no prayer being answered, and enemies receiving strength, yet he filled himself with this intense, ecstatic and exultant pleasure.

How To Allow Joy To Rule Over Your Life

Cherry ice cream makes me very happy. Blue jeans that fit make me very happy. Children who don't argue in the car make me very happy. But, smiling while I'm grieving, being able to hug a power hungry, prideful sheep who has hurt me, helping someone that has hurt me and having indescribable excitement when my world is falling apart, now that is the joy of the Lord. But how do you get this part of the fruit of love to grow?

Joy comes as you begin to make a choice to let the love shed abroad in your hearts as Romans 5:5 says, move in to the practical side where it starts to be seen by others. It starts when you are moved by love and when you see the best in every person. When your mouth speaks no evil of any man, joy comes and overtakes your life. Joy does not speak evil of anyone Jesus died for.

You see as you walk more and more into the will of God for your life, your joy becomes greater and greater because you are walking into the light of the Lord and this makes joy work for you always.

In Acts 16 we see what joy is when someone is in the will of God upon their lives. Joy here looks at Christ and not the situation. Joy says if I am still doing what the lord said to do it does not matter whether the wind blows or the enemies accuse me.

See here that joy does not just trust the Lord will deliver you from the problem, although he will AND HE WILL, but in that God who is above all says, I am ok with him and I am in him. That gives you joy when you know, I am doing what I am supposed to do so nothing against me can move me though it comes. See, joy says I will stay put in the Lord in the midst of trouble. I know I will be delivered but my joy is not based on that fact but on the Lord and I having a relationship. Joy goes deeper than happiness. It reaches the core of our relationship with a higher power, The Lord Jesus Christ Himself!

Listen, you know God will deliver you, that is His nature but your joy is not based on that, it is based on you being one with the Lord. That's it. You are not rejoicing just because he will come and beat your enemies. You are rejoicing because you are known by him and you are in him. That is how joy takes over your life in the day of trouble.

In verse 25 it says:

But about midnight Paul and Silas were praying and singing hymns to God, and the prisoners were listening to them.

No matter what happened, Satan could try to put them in prison, persecute them, make life miserable for them but they never lost their song. They were in the Lord and they knew it. Their song was not because they were trying to bribe God into delivering them. No not at all. When you never lose your song you are walking in God's will. That's the first step to getting an overflow of joy.

This is not a trust in the Lord that says he will deliver me, no, that will be happiness because happiness always carries a reason but here joy carries no other reason except "I am in the Lord!"

It All Starts By A Choice

Joy is a choice. It's not a feeling; it is a choice you can make today. Tell yourself today that you will enjoy. Pat yourself on the back and shout, "something good is going to happen to me today!" Habakkuk remained strong knowing he was in the Lord. He knew the Lord would deliver them but did not know when or how. He also knew that his enemies had gained momentum yet he felt joy in him based upon his relationship with God and not just on the benefits of protection that God could have promised him.

In our modern world, Habakkuk might have said it this way:

"Though there is no food in the refrigerator, and there is no money in the account, though the sickness gets worse, and the pain persists, though my children are on drugs, and my spouse does not appreciate me, yet I will rejoice in the Lord, I will be joyful in God my Saviour."

This would be a big situation but Habakkuk says he will trust him. He knew the Lord would deliver him but so far it did not look like it so he could only be happy in whom he was in God, His prophet.

You can decide to rejoice just because you are known by him. You are not just a worm with no direction. You are his child so be joyous. Shout for joy not because of the benefits you get but because God is your father. That is pure joy with no strings attached.

Joy is in a nutshell based upon your relationship with God. When your relationship with God is up, your joy will be on the up. This is the secret to joy and you can change your relationship with your maker today. Your relationship with the Lord Jesus can change today. Speak to Him; tell him you are ready to get deeper with him. Tell the Holy Spirit you are ready for a deeper walk. Tell God, this is the time for you to go deeper than before in your walk with him. He is ready to answer with a yes.

This is also the way peace comes over your life. As mentioned before joy and peace affect the spirit man and goes out to influence the soul and the body. Joy and peace work together. They are parts of a bigger fruit of love just like all the other six which include gladness, longsuffering, patience etc.

Though some parts of this fruit are different in the way they work, what you see with joy can also be seen with peace. This is because they fall under the same group that is directly linked to the spirit man hence their concentration on the relationship with God.

Expect Joy!

Expect good things, be at ease and enjoy life but the primary aspect of joy is that it contains no strings attached. It is unconditional for it is directly linked to its mother, love, just like peace is. However you need to expect it to take over your life on a daily basis.

Yes, expectation is the mother of manifestation and it shows one's faith in the Lord but should never be a prerequisite to rejoicing in the Lord. If that becomes the case, it is no longer joy. It turns into happiness which relies on circumstances being right first before it manifests. By this I am not implying that happiness is all bad. No I am not implying that at all for it is evident from the revelation that we have gotten so far that happiness does not contain joy and joy does not necessarily contain happiness. Joy can contain happiness but sometimes it might not.

To let joy flow, start by a mindset that says I can do it. It is possible. Joy is in my reach. I am ready to enjoy. My joy is full. Nothing moves me. I expect joy to rule my life and that is the great choice to be made.

If You Have Joy, You Possess Strength
Nehemiah 8: 10

"The joy of the Lord is your strength."

The absence of joy spells weakness so anyone who can steal your joy will also have access to your power. If Satan can steal your joy, he can steal your power. If Satan can steal your joy, he can steal your strength. If Satan can steal your joy, he can steal your health. It is important for us to learn to preserve joy. If you lose your joy you lose your strength. If you lose your joy you lose your health. Ever been in a situation where things just took a dive in your life and you actually became very physically tired? You didn't even have the strength to try and fix the situation. Why does this happen? The devil has stolen your joy. No joy, no strength.

Before Adam and Eve lost their health and sickness, they lost their link with God so joy departed. Their focus on God was affected when they allowed the devil to steal their joy. Do you see what a bad relationship with God can bring you to? As believers we are those already in a relationship with God. All we need to do is to sharpen that relationship.

Adam and Eve removed themselves from God's instructions and affected their relationship to the extent where the devil stole their joy so they lost their Garden. Their home was taken. Their pride was taken.

We cannot keep our strength if we lose our joy. This strength is really the Lord's strength in us when we allow joy to come through a deeper relationship with the Lord Jesus. Some might have wanted me to talk about some kind of way that we can increase joy that has nothing to do with a relationship with a higher power, Jesus Christ, but that would be a lie. I am here to give only the truth. There is no joy outside the Lord Jesus and that is a fact.

When real joy which is from the Lord impregnates your whole being it turns your weakness upside down and replaces it with God's strength. Remember the scripture says;

"...Those who wait upon the Lord shall renew their strength..."

Isaiah 40:31

The word renew there is the word **'*exchange*'** so the scripture would read:

"...Those who wait upon the Lord shall *exchange their strength* **for God's strength..."**

You see there that when joy is on you God's strength becomes your strength and no enemy can win here. God's ability becomes your ability. That is the joy that the Lord gives. It gives you strength for your weakness.

Apostle Paul said it well:

"...My strength is made perfect in weakness..."

2 Corinthians 12:9

How? He was a man of joy and God is your strength when you keep this joy in you. This joy as aforementioned is not happiness. Happiness is included in joy but joy in not necessarily in happiness. These are two different things. One requires feelings and is dependent upon circumstances but the other does not care about circumstances for it looks not at things which are seen.

Look, the Apostle Paul says,

"...Looking not at things which are seen for things which are seen are temporal..."

2 Corinthians 4:18

The word 'temporal' there is proskairos which means subject to change meaning that Apostle Paul's joy came out of his spirit and flowed outside by faith and was not caused by circumstances but went over the circumstances. It looked at Jesus and not the circumstances to the extent that Apostle Paul was not looking at all he was going through, which could have given him sadness, he uttered those famous words of someone who was more than a conqueror;

"...None of these things move me..."

Acts 20:24

That was joy speaking and not circumstances. See, never lose your joy. Joy comes out by faith and you can decide for it to become an ever flowing stream and not for it to be occasional. I made a decision to be joyous and not to be moved.

Notice something about the Apostle Paul here. When you analyse Apostle Paul's life, you can easily say, I want to be like him. I have seen many that want to be like him, that cherish the chance if obtained to enter into his shoes, but the man suffered.

The question however is this; how did he get through all those things that we read in the word? How could he say he had joy when we know the horrific things he went through? How can there be any joy in being stoned once like he did, several times shipwrecked and whipped on his back more than thirty eight times. His back was often under the whip just because he uttered the name of Jesus. He had not stolen anything. He had not committed adultery or some crazy sin but still they stoned him and caused him to go through a lot yet he was full of joy and because of this he could utter the words;

"...None of these things move me..."

Where did he actually get his strength? The joy of the Lord gave him strength. The joy that is pushed out from within and not by circumstances gives you strength. The joy that is obtained when one is a child of God and increased with a deeper relationship with God gave Apostle Paul strength.

Don't Be A Wimp

Believers have turned into wimps to such an extent that the moment little trouble comes, Christians backslide. They leave church. They gossip about their leaders regardless of what the Lord said the conduct of a real Christian ought to be. The moment a few wrong words are shared to them or criticism comes, all kinds of things will come out of their lives. A little pressure pressed on them, they give up. Just a little pressure they bend, yet the Apostle Paul went through worse and to compare it, will be out of sorts for a real believer. You need to stand tall in the Lord knowing that as long as you're in him and He is in you, your joy will be full.

God wants a Christianity of joy that is not motivated

by circumstances. This is the life believers ought to live. In this kind of life pain is nothing. With this kind of joy diseases are nothing. With this kind of joy problems are nothing. Gossip is nothing, persecution and all the trials of life are nothing. God wants loving and joy filled Christians who could be a contribution to this life.

Rejoice Always

Philippians 4:4 says,

"Rejoice in the Lord always. I will say it again: Rejoice!"

How often am I to rejoice? How often should this joy be on me per day? Do I have it in the morning or when I face problems only? How often should I have this joy? You know the answer, **Always!**

You are to rejoice always, because "joy" is the easiest fruit to lose. It needs to be obtained every time. Joy is attached to your strength, so the devil is hunting for your strength every minute, so you cannot afford to lose it. You should have it always. Rejoice ALWAYS!

You can't live off the joy you had yesterday. Joy can give you strength only when you possess it today, this hour, this minute and this second. If you had joy last week, that joy will not give you strength today. Joy can only give you strength today, if you have it today. This is why you must rejoice always, always and not sometimes. Joy is the easiest fruit to lose so God requires it to be always.

You might say, "I don't feel like rejoicing." God didn't say, "Rejoice, only if you feel like it." This has nothing to do with feeling. This is not happiness; it is joy with nothing to do with feelings or happenings around you. God didn't say, "Rejoice sometimes when you feel like it". No! He said, "Rejoice always." Obviously, God knows that you don't feel like rejoicing always. Yet you need to rejoice always because if you don't then you will be in weakness.

Look at what David says;

Psalm 149:5

"Let the saints be joyful in glory; Let them sing aloud on their beds."

There is an instruction here, even on our beds we should rejoice regardless of the happenings around us. Joy should fill your heart no matter what the enemy wants to do to your life. No matter what the enemy throws at you, sing even in your bed. Rejoice wherever you are. This is what David was trying to communicate here. You also notice that all these scriptures are going on the direction of joy being based on the relationship that you have with the Lord and not on what is happening around you. What is happening around you matters to God but joy hinges on what relationship you have with the Lord.

Look at all the problems Paul was going through, yet he still spoke boldly because of Joy. Joy gives strength and gives power to the weak. The weak exchange their weakness for the strength of God. God takes their weakness and in exchange gives them strength that ushers in boldness.

Apostle Paul did not care about what he did not have. He knew there was strength in him because of the joy of the Lord. He knew boldness was for him.

Read 2 Corinthians 7:4:

"Great is my boldness of speech toward you, great is my boasting on your behalf. I am filled with comfort. I am exceedingly joyful in all tribulations.

Apostle Paul was not just joyful, he was exceedingly joyful. Now that is extreme joy. That is intense, ecstatic and exultant pleasure in the Lord. Even in all persecutions he was getting from people, he could not get any problems; the man was ok when things around him were not going well at all. You see, you need to remove the mind that things have to be good for you to enjoy life now. Enjoy life regardless of what is happening.

Never Stop

I know people normally are stopped from following their heart's desire because one or two things are not working well in their lives. This is not the best step to take. Enjoy life right now to the extent that the thing which would have stopped you will meet you on the way to your destiny. Nothing on this earth should ever stop you from getting to the level of joy you desire.

I can think of a lot of things that stopped me from having joy. The devil stole my joy until I was left with happiness and at that time there was nothing to be happy about so I was miserable. Those things that I fretted about, kept me disappointed for years, BUT now that I have all those things that I desired, I realize that I wasted years. If I had kept my joy I would have achieved more than half of what I have right now. I allowed my joy to leave me because of some few things that were happening. It affected my relationship with the Lord and that made me go for years thinking of what I did not have instead of rejoicing, regardless of what I did not have, so that when those things came I would have achieved more since I would be having the strength to do other things that were in my reach.

James 1:2 says,

"Consider it pure joy, my brothers, whenever you face trials of many kinds."

Why is James telling us to count it pure joy whenever we face trials? Because joy gives you strength to fight your trials, and if you'll fight the trials, you will overcome.

James continues,

"Perseverance must finish its work so that you may be mature and complete, not lacking anything" (chapter 1:4).

Maturity as you see here is linked to the relationship one has with the Lord. Maturity is measured inside the Lord's confines not by the material things you have or the happenings around you. You see, James has in mind maturity when he faced problems and not just victory. He had victory over trials in his mind alright but he had a greater thing which is maturity in the Lord that he served. That is the other focus of joy. So by rejoicing, James was going to mature in the Lord and also overcome but his primary goal was maturity in the Lord.

Full Joy Or Less

There is full joy and there is half, small, little and even no joy, but for joy to be described as full it depends upon other parts of the fruit being obtained and aiding it, hence this book. Remember Apostle Paul talks of full joy.

"...that your joy may be full..."

If Apostle Paul tells people that he was sending something so that their joy could be full that shows us the same joy can be half full or less than half full. Apostle Paul's statement however, shows that there is such a level where your joy can actually be full and also that this level is available to believers and can be obtained and also that believers can expect to move into this joy. This is the reality of Apostle Paul. It is his revelation and it should also be your revelation if you want this full joy.

Remember earlier on we discovered that we are spirit, we possess a soul and live in a body and also that these principles are grouped in three parts that take over the whole person spirit, soul and body and produce joy unspeakable.

These three groups are in connection with the

spirit, soul and body. This fruit controls your spirit, controls your soul and controls your body. By now you know, we are spirit beings, who possess a soul and live in a body. If you look again at Galatians 5:22-23, you will notice that the first two parts of love as the fruit of the Spirit **joy** and **peace** are always the basic control of our spirit man. If your spirit man is right with God, you will always sense love which promotes **joy** and **peace** over your spirit.

After that there are three called **longsuffering, kindness and goodness** which have everything to do with the fruit of the Spirit growing forth and controlling your soul. Your soul consists of mind, will and emotions, so longsuffering, kindness and goodness control your mind, will and emotions. They control your soul. The last three **faithfulness, gentleness and self-control** speak of control that rises from your spirit through the Holy Spirit upon **your body** and master it into submission to the will of the Spirit and in turn, the control of all these three areas by the Spirit bring joy. When one manages to follow the revelation in the word with regards to these areas they will possess full joy.

Someone might say "I believe I have this joy but sometimes I know it's not what I really want it to be, so what should I do?" That is a simple question with a simple answer. All you need is to get to a level where you understand all the parts of this fruit of the Spirit called Love so as to get all the parts rooted in you and you practicing them, then you can stand and say I have what Apostle Paul had, full joy, and I can do all things and nothing moves me. This is the level God wants his children to reach.

God did not intend for us to be angry or be angered every time and walk dejected, frustrated and bored. God wants the best to happen and tomorrow to worry about its own problems and not the believer. That's why he says:

"...Tomorrow will take care of its own..."

Matthew 6:34

He also said:

"...be careful for nothing..."

Philippians 4:6

In other words he is saying **"...do not be anxious..."** He is saying do not worry. Remember what he said to us about worrying and not finding sleep due to the fretting. Always thinking what tomorrow might bring. God is against fretting and is for joy filling us, **always,** that problems of life are not permitted to rule us or for us to worry about them. That is God. He is against worry for he knows worrying is the absence of joy and the absence of joy is the presence of weakness.

God even throws in a question about worrying to those who have lost their joy and those who rely on happenings.

"What can you do by worrying? Will you be able to add a cubit to your stature by it?"

Matthew 6:27

God says you do not need to worry and shows that worry will not add anything to you. In fact it takes away from you. Worry has no positive attributes except negative ones. Worry kills but Joy gives life for the joy of the Lord really is strength.

When my husband started moving deeper into the healing and prophetic anointing where he called out strangers by name and giving them intimate details about their lives coupled with what was to happen in their lives with great accuracy, persecution mounted against us. Some did not understand him, some mocked, some thought something was afoot and yet some thought the devil was at work. At first it hurt but when the Lord told us to take into consideration all the parts of the fruit of love that aid joy, nothing moves us anymore.

In fact my husband is filled with great joy when he meets one who does not believe and at the same time he feels for them. He has in him a push to get these people to know the ability of God to speak.

The same happens with regards to healing and we have seen healings like never before. In the crusades we are sent by the Lord to do around the world, we have seen deaf ears opening, blind eyes opening, the dead being raised, wheelchair bound people coming out of wheelchairs, short limps growing. We have seen a lot of miracles. All that evidence.

In fact, in St Lucia people went to doctors after the healing line and found out the truth of the healing ministry. Cancer disappeared and doctors confirmed it. Many ailments were confirmed by doctors yet we had opposition coming from all corners including the so called Christians. In times past we could have been very depressed but because my husband and I have learnt the truth about joy from the Lord, and that it has nothing to do with happenings and that it is a truth to what the Lord is and who the Lord is, we are really not moved. Here I mean, not even an inch. We are relaxed in the Lord. Our joy is very full that our enemies are just wasting time. In fact they are advertising for us.

We are not moved an inch by opposition, we feed on it!

Like Paul, my husband was told by God;

"None of these things should move you..."

As long as you know you are in the right path with God what others say should never move you. My husband was never moved. I also jumped in and was never discouraged and now no one can discourage us. We are not fazed anymore. You cannot disappoint a person with the joy of the Lord. You may try but they will not be moved.

We are now even moving high in anointing because of the joy we have. We are not looking at the things that are taking place around us. We are set on the course we must follow. Never are we going back on our word to work for God and in whatever you know is your destiny, you should not be moved. You should never be stopped. Keep moving forward, this is your life so no one has a right to stop your progress.

Gossip should not stop you. People lying about you should never stop you or your joy. Never be stopped. We have a lot of success the Lord has given us but we also have many who lie about us and those who also listen to those who lie about us. However all this does not stop us. It gives us fuel to move because we have joy. Joy has caused the lies spoken against me and my family and my businesses to turn into adverts.

The lies and the gossip do not affect me so when people see me they see joy when they expect to see sorrow. I can safely tell any person that I AM HAVING A BLAST!

I am having the time of my life. And nothing can stop me. I am like Habakkuk;

"Though the fig tree does not bud and there are no grapes on the vines, though the olive crop fails and the fields produce no food, though there are no sheep in the pen and no cattle in the stalls, YET..."

See this again; how can Habakkuk put **"YET..."** when he had nothing to show for anything? He was in serious hardships. In serious problems yet the word YET exists in his mouth. See what he said;

He says, **"Yet I will REJOICE IN THE LORD, I will be JOYFUL IN GOD MY SAVIOR" (3:18).**

Some can say, "You can enjoy because God has blessed you with material things", but they would be mistaken in that I did not start where I am right now.

I remember when we did not have anything in our life. I remember when there was no money, no good thing that one can be glad about but because I adopted steps to be joyous like Habakkuk 3:17 says, I rejoiced and now that God has blessed us with material things, that means something because of joy. See if material things come to you when you don't have joy they will be a disease to you. They will be a big problem. However we still have challenges the devil throws at us. Other problems arise and many lie and talk against you and some try to bring lawsuits against you and some needs still do arise but the joy of the Lord controls my life so I win every time.

I do not look at any of those things and I don't have joy because I am just expecting God to do something for me. I know he will but that is not the primary goal. My goal is my relationship with the Lord, my maturity in God.

No one can get me low in life. No gossip, no lie, no financial problem, no opposition, no factor can get me to lose my joy because if you lose joy, you lose your strength.

What others do or say about you does not matter, after all they do not know where God has brought you from. You and you alone know you were saved by God and know where the Lord sent you to and that he has saved you from a might long way, way far that only God matters. Never suffer from approval addiction that you want to make everyone happy. Make God happy, that's it.

Remember in Acts the Lord said;

"...I have delivered from the people..."

You see sometimes it is people that possess people and not just demons to the extent where God says "...I have delivered you from the people..."

Don't suffer from approval addiction. Only be an addict to be approved of God. That is what matters. You can say, 'How do you do it?' Keep your joy. You don't work for people, you work for God and he is ready to bring you forth to another level if you just keep your joy.

Join Joy with Peace

No circumstance should stop you from your dreams. Go for your dreams. Aim for your dreams regardless of any obstacle trying to remove you from your way. Many obstacles present a challenge that will cause you to say, 'I will only do this if this or that thing is out of the way'. That beloved is a way the devil tries to move you from your destiny. With joy you will understand that problems gravitate towards their solution.

Circumstances should not remove you from your joy so when you see them come towards you, your attitude should be that of someone who says, I am not moved and I can be a solution to this problem. This is the reality that we need to have in order to keep our joy. However joy needs to be full as aforementioned so we need to look at other parts of the fruit to see how we can aid joy and move it to the 'full' level.

Notice joy and peace are partners that are directly linked to your spirit so they work closely together. All the other parts of the fruits also work with joy and peace but joy and peace are closely linked to the spirit man so it is necessary to talk about their link so one can understand how full joy can be achieved easily.

Get your relationship with the Lord to be strong and concentrate on your maturity in him and not just on his ability to save to the uttermost. Yes he will save but your focus should be on the Lord because it is your nature as a believer.

A cow moos, a cat mews and a dog barks, but a believer also has a nature. A believer is filled with joy. How often? **Always!**

CHAPTER THREE

The Force Of Peace

Peace is a force. It is an explosion of power. It is a release of the fire of God!

When believers hear the word 'peace' they think of something quiet with no energy in it but here they would be wrong because the Bible speaks of peace as a conquering force and a killing machine. Peace is a dangerous partner to Joy. It is the kill switch. It is by far not fragile. It is an explosion of God's ability that will send your enemies packing and your pain to smithereens.

Notice Romans 16: 20 here;

"...The God of peace will crush Satan under your feet shortly..."

How can Apostle Paul confuse these statements? He mentions peace and crushing in the same vein and then says the one who is peaceful will crush his enemies. How? This is because peace is not fragile. It is a great force. It is an explosion. Many who read Galatians 5 think they already know peace but that is a fallacy. Peace has bullets in it. It carries grenades of power.

What Then Is This Peace Really?

Greek - *eirene*, which is the word for peace here as God called it, comes when something is done by us in an **irenic** way, which is being done in a way that helps find common ground, creates understanding and appreciation, or soothes sore points of dispute. Paul was calling Christians to be irenic using God's definition for it though. Remember he was saying there is something that peace does to find common ground, create understanding and appreciation and also soothing sore points of dispute and that way is through the force that crushes the enemy under the believer's feet.

Apostle Paul here could have used a different word to speak about God. He could have said the God almighty will crush Satan and we would have taken it and agreed with it. He could have said the omnipotent God will crush Satan but instead he said the God of peace who should be silent is also going to crush my enemies under my feet.

You see if you don't understand peace you would think that the manifestation of God as peace will cause quietness to come or calmness to come before a crushing but not an explosion first. Surely not explosion yet Apostle Paul joins peace and crushing together. This then is not normal peace. Normal peace would be silent but this is loaded with fire power. This is the peace of God which is the partner to faith. It is not silent but causes silence after it crushes the enemy. It is not like the world peace.

Notice the Lord's own words:

John 14:27 and He says:

"Peace I leave with you. My peace I give to you, not as the world gives do I give to you".

This is not normal peace. It is peace that is explosive and the Lord says this is the peace we have. Wow! It's not a natural peace at all. It is supernatural peace. It contains a force behind it. Peace is therefore a spiritual supernatural force that is supposed to transform this whole earth. It is a force with a lot of power to aid joy and transform the worst of people.

Peace Protects

"...The peace of God shall keep your heart..."

Philippians 4:7

The word 'keep' here means to mount guard like a sentinel or to post spies at the gate of your heart. It also means putting an army around your heart so you remain calm to the surprise of your enemies. This peace hems you in and protects your heart and if you embrace it nothing will offend you. Like a mighty garrison, peace encircles you with a great occupying force. It cannot and will not be denied. You do not just maintain joy because of who you are in Christ.

Peace aids joy in that it brings calmness to joy. Joy is excited because you are connected to God regardless of what happens, peace says I am protected so when one adds peace to joy, joy then becomes strengthened because it now knows that it is hemmed in and that the heart is protected. Your spirit then is strengthened when such happens.

When My Son Was Diagnosed

One of my sons was born with one kidney and that would make any mom cringe in fear. It is something that will shatter all your confidence yet the peace of the Lord was upon me. There was a soothing in me. The doctor said he saw one kidney and we said no, they were two to his face. We went for further tests and the report kept coming back that they could only see one. We had peace and this peace mounted guards on our hearts that our joy in the time of trouble was full to the destruction of the devil and the devil had to remove his hand. You see there are two things that you need to know for healing miracles to take place. There are facts which we are told by medical practitioners and then there is truth which is in the word of God. You are the one who chooses whether you want to follow the facts or follow the truth in the word of God that confirms that we were healed by His stripes. With no medicine, my son now has two kidneys. Peace destroyed the plans of the enemy and aided my joy.

Notice that the peace of God works in the spirit just like joy but aids joy so it would look like joy and peace are the same thing when in actual fact they are really not. Apostle Paul listed them in order here and in their groups. He was attesting in a way that peace is a partner to joy. Peace hems the believer in and mounts guard on the heart that you are never surprised or perplexed. Joy says I will rejoice regardless of what happens and when the peace is there then joy knows too that my rejoicing is well in my heart for the heart is protected regardless of anything coming against you.

How To Get This Peace

"Thou wilt keep him in perfect peace, whose mind is stayed on Thee: because he trusteth in Thee. Trust ye in the LORD for ever: for in the LORD JEHOVAH is everlasting strength"

Isaiah 26:3-4

The word "stayed" in verse 3 means to lean upon or take hold of. It is a choice to lean on the Lord and stay focussed on Him and that is what joy does too. Do you see how it is inter-twinned? When you lean on the Lord peace comes and peace protects your heart. Do you see the link? Rejoice always first and there will be peace on your heart, there will be a posting of guards around your heart. It is not the other way around here. Rejoice and let the peace of God mount a sentinel over your life and when that happens, no weapon formed against you shall prosper for you are hemmed in and joy is in you.

See what Isaiah says in 41:10

"Fear thou not; for I am with thee: be not dismayed; for I am thy God: I will strengthen thee; yea, I will help thee; yea, I will uphold thee with the right hand of my righteousness"

Do you see that there is a keeping here which is a joint part of peace and joy? I will strengthen you means there will be peace and I am with thee shows that joy has an anchor and when peace joins joy then there is great joy.

See you need to take a hold of Jesus and trust Him with your struggles, cast your cares upon him for it is in Him that you will find answers. You see here that joy does not major on how the Lord will deliver you, peace does. What a combination. What a partnership!

With peace, you are not afraid. You do not fear anything. You do not care about anything for all your cares are cast upon the Lord. This is a surrender of problems to a higher Lord Jesus who can do something about them. Scripture says;

"...Be careful for nothing..."

Philippians 4:6

This scripture does not end there it says:

"...But in everything by prayer and supplication with thanksgiving let your requests be made known unto God. And the peace of God, which

passeth all understanding, shall keep your hearts and minds through Christ Jesus..."

Philippians 4:6-7

Here it says this peace only comes when I make my requests to him and believe he is going to answer, so peace survives when there is hope for a miracle. Joy survives even when there is no hope for a miracle. However explosive joy happens also when peace comes in. Remember happiness does not have joy but joy may contain happiness. This scripture also says this peace surpasses all understanding. This means that whatever doubts I might have will be eradicated and blown into pieces because of this peace. This peace cancels all reason and focuses on a miracle, so to keep this peace I need to hope the more and act upon the word of God I have believed.

The Solution To Doubt

The solution to doubt, discouragement, fretting, and worrying, is to give them all to the Lord in prayer, trusting in Him to answer them according to His perfect will. In other words peace relies on faith and faith is not just believing but acting upon what one believes. If you believe God has already answered your prayer then act like it and don't fret. Be calm if you have faith and your peace will become evident. It is in calmness that faith is seen in one's life. One is not moved when they have faith. They know they have joy and they know peace is there too.

This controls the spirit of man. It sharpens the

spirit of man and causes it to be sensitive to God. In short, peace is the lubricant for joy because it helps joy to flow freely.

One of the manifestations that faith is in a person's life is peace. Someone striving in the flesh to do something is different from someone in peace who just flows along with what God wants to do and also know God will answer prayers. Here there is no effort from the human point of view. There is a world of difference. Therefore, peace is also the result of faith.

Peace Is A Way Not A Condition

The Bible calls peace a way. Luke 2:79 says;

To give light to those who sit in darkness and the shadow of death. To guide our feet into the way of peace.

Here we see that peace is referred to as a way. Many think of it as a condition yet the word says it is also a way and a way leads to something or somewhere. Now his prophecy was about John the forerunner of Jesus Christ our Lord but here is a wonderful truth. The phrase says to guide our feet into the way of peace. Do we think of peace as a way? We think of peace as a condition. However, he says peace is a road. It is a path to something. A road to a certain place.

Therefore, peace is a roadway, a way that we walk in as we leave other roads for there is danger in every road. Only the road of peace has an army that can lead you to joy. This path is found by those who follow the way of the Lord for peace is also connected to the will of God since it is connected to influencing the spirit man. No other place is more powerful than to be in God's perfect will. When we are in God's perfect will, we are in the shadow of the Most High or the secret place of the Most High that David talked about. We will be under the epikaizo of God where the highest power of God exists. That shows us that the power of peace comes when we get deeper in prayer that everything in us agrees with the heart beat of God. Peace therefore is well connected to the heart beat of God.

This cancels out fear. Peace is the opposite of fear. Both are roads but the road of peace is incomparable to the bad road of fear for fear is full of demonic forces. When you move in the peace highway fear runs!

No wonder the bible says;

You shall not be afraid of the arrow that flies by day or the pestilence that walk at night.

Psalm 91:5-6

Peace is a force, peace is a matter, which can be seen, and peace is a road that we walk in as we navigate the avenues of life. It is the road to joy. It is a magnetic way for joy. It leads to something greater than the issues one is going through. It is a force.

Throw your problems to Jesus he knows how to deal with them. When police knock at your door with summons, send for the army guarding your heart and you will see what happens. When the doctor speaks to you about the diagnosis let the ears of your soldiers who guard your heart listen instead of you and you will see what will happen to that report. When doubts and fear knock on the door of your heart, send Jesus to answer them. The soldiers mounting the door of your heart will answer. When the bailiffs knock at your door, send the garrison on your heart to answer. Let every problem that knocks at your door be met by the army that hems you in. Let the cushioning peace you have answer them. I assure you this peace will know what to say and how to respond. It is very simple. Do you see that?

Trust in the Lord, wait on Him in prayer, and He promises to give you the strength you need to protect you.

Who is among you that feareth the LORD, that obeyeth the voice of His servant, that walketh in darkness, and hath no light? Let him trust in the name of the LORD, and stay upon his God. Behold, all ye that kindle a fire, that compass yourselves about with sparks: walk in the light of your fire, and in the sparks that ye have kindled. This shall ye have of Mine hand; ye shall lie down in sorrow.

Isaiah 50:10-11

As said before the word "stay" in verse 10 means "to support one's self; lean, rely on, rest on." If you want perfect peace even in the midst of trials

- when your way is dark and you can't understand why the Lord is allowing certain afflictions in your life, don't make your own way. Peace becomes the way. Walk the way of peace. It is a way and not just a condition. When a way is not evident or when a way is not being seen peace will do wonders. It is a way to walk in and when one walks in it, the joy of the Lord becomes stimulated. In the way of peace there is calmness for the power peace has can crush enemies and move your problems into nothingness. Don't look at the problems when you are walking in this path instead, look to the Lord and His Word. Then trust in Him and lean on Him. Let Jesus be your everything. Let Him be your peace, your strength, your refuge, shield, and your fortress. Let Him be your LORD!

First Be At Peace With Yourself

You cannot give what you do not have. Only when peace rests in our hearts, we are cool and calm in the things of God and in the will of God that we can bring peace to people and then can we have peace with others. Be at peace with yourself first. When we are in strife, we will bring strife to people. We cannot give what we do not have. When one has peace, only then can they distribute peace.

Notice that if you have this kind of explosive force on the inside, any disturbance from the outside cannot hurt you. It will not happen!

Don't Worry about Anything

Look at these promises of peace and joy that show the interlink and also the benefits of having joy and walking in peace to get to joy. See how the Lord is set on blessing his kids with full joy.

"Be anxious about nothing; but in everything by prayer and supplication with thanksgiving let your requests be made known unto God. And the peace of God, which passes all understanding, shall keep your hearts and minds through Christ Jesus."

Philippians 4:6-7

"Cast all your anxiety on him because he cares for you."

1 Peter 5:7

"All things work together for good to them that love God and are the called according to his purpose."

Romans 8:28

"Thou wilt keep him in perfect peace, whose mind is stayed on thee: because he trusts in thee."

Isaiah 26:3

Do you see how the dedication of the Lord to you as his child works? He is expecting the best for you every time and promises safety after safety that will give your enemies a heart attack. God here is showing you that he is here to give you rest. No need to fret, worry or be perturbed. You cannot get any surprises he is showing you that he loves you.

Look at the depth of God's love through his word

here;

"These things have I spoken unto you, that in me ye might have peace. In the world ye shall have tribulation; but be of good cheer, for I have overcome the world."

John 16:33

Here he even says be of good joy because you have peace. That is another interlink that is very plain. He expects joy because you are at peace with him. Peace here is thrown in and joy also to show you that joy is complete when it carries other parts of the fruit called love.

There is safety for the righteous that their joy can grow with no limits or boundaries. No need to walk with a long face. You are the child of the Lord and so you have the protection of the Lord which is the best in the universe and every other place created or not created you can ever find. Your peace is bigger than any other peace because you are in the Lord who is great.

See what **Proverbs 18:10, Deuteronomy 33:12, Psalms 4:8, Psalm 27:1,**

"The name of the Lord is a strong tower; the righteous run into it, and is safe."

And of Benjamin he said, "The beloved of the Lord shall dwell in safety by him; and the Lord shall cover him all the day long, and he shall dwell between his shoulders."

"I will both lay me down in peace, and sleep:

for thou, Lord, only makest me dwell in safety."

"The Lord is my light and my salvation; whom shall I fear? The Lord is the strength of my life; of whom shall I be afraid?"

The book of Psalm also presents a host of scriptures that show the peace and joy of the Lord in motion to protect the believer. It is a book that a believer who wants encouragement and revelation on how the Lord is set on maximising their joy should read.

Just look up these scriptures and pour your heart on them. The whole book of the Psalms is a bullion of words that stimulate your faith. Remember a man of faith is a man of peace. Act upon the words of God you believe and see what peace you will walk in.

You will be as cool as an ice cube!

Look at these scriptures for a while before we move on to other parts where we control the soul and then to how the body can be controlled in order to maximise the joy you deserve.

"Because thou hast made the Lord, which is my refuge, even the most High, thy habitation; there shall no evil befall thee, neither shall any plague come nigh thy dwelling."

Psalm 91:9-10

"He shall not be afraid of evil tidings: his heart is fixed, trusting in the Lord."

Psalm 112:7

"The Lord shall preserve thee from all evil: he shall preserve thy soul. The Lord shall preserve thy going out and thy coming in from this time forth, and even for evermore."

Psalms 121:7-8

The book of Proverbs has some good nuggets as well;

"But whoso hearkeneth unto me shall dwell safely, and shall be quiet from fear of evil."

Proverbs 1:33

"When thou liest down, thou shalt not be afraid: yea, thou shalt lie down, and thy sleep shall be sweet."

Proverbs 3:2

"But whoso hearkeneth unto me shall dwell safely, and shall be quiet from fear of evil."

Proverbs 1:33

Did you see that? God is intentionally making it known that he would put his reputation on the line for you. Here says he would protect you. You will be hidden from fear. Your days will be peaceful. That is the God of peace and Joy. This is the God of peace who will crush your enemies under your foot.

How? Enemies attack where there is fear. You know that in zoology they say dogs never attack anyone who does not release a fear hormone.

They sense the fear hormone then attack so those who do not fear will dwell safely and not fear so demons will not succeed!

Be At Peace With God Also

The peace of God has a certain quality about it. In the world, peace is a condition of being in harmony one with another in the natural. In the kingdom of God peace directly relates to harmony with the source Himself, the Almighty God the Father.

See this: Ephesians 2:13-14,

We have peace with God because of the blood of the cross "For he himself (Christ Jesus) is our peace..."

So peace in the bible is a state or a position of being in God. Do you see again that peace has just linked itself to joy for joy rejoices because it's in God before it looks for a miracle? However, peace looks at the miracle for its well versed in the word to the point that it knows of God's protection.

This is the doctrine from which comes the practice of manifesting peace with God because we live as ones who have peace with God. Jesus Christ's blood was shed to pay for every error of mankind (1John 2:2). Because all of our errors have been cleansed by his blood, we have been justified. This is why we have peace with God. We have been justified, so when we see others that are attacking us we quickly relax and we don't take offence, knowing we were like them before but now grace has given us peace with God so we also need to forgive and not react.

Peace knows the way. When problems are too many it knows the way, for peace is the way out of problems.

In Christ we have safety, security, prosperity and felicity. Jehovah is all these promises to us through Christ. Since God is now for us, who or what could be against us? (Romans 8:31) We have peace with God through our Lord Jesus Christ.

The book of Proverbs concurs:

"Be not afraid of sudden fear, neither of the desolation of the wicked, when it cometh. For the Lord shall be thy confidence, and shall keep thy foot from being taken."

Proverbs 3:25-26

You see God is our refuge and strength, a very present help in trouble as Psalm 46:1 says. He shall cover you with his feathers, and under his wings we shall dwell. His truth shall be YOUR shield and buckler. You shall not be afraid of the terror by night; nor of the arrow that flieth by day; nor of the pestilence that walks in darkness; nor of the destruction that wasteth at noonday that is the testimony of Psalm 91:4-6.

The writer had experienced God's protection. He had seen the great protection of the Lord to the extent that it was very plain to him that God brings peace when we pray and decide to live a prayed up life. The writer had a revelation that when we trust in God, God would bring this explosive peace. See what Proverbs says;

"The fear of man bringeth a snare: but whoso putteth his trust in the Lord shall be safe."

Proverbs 29:25

Isaiah explains it even deeper here in Isaiah 43:2. He shows that the peace we are talking about here is not a weak one but a burning one. He got a revelation that when you pass through the waters, he will be with you; and through the rivers, they shall not overflow thee: when you walk through the fire, you shall not be burned; neither shall the flame kindle upon thee.

What Isaiah was looking at was peace that was different. Many when they see peace they think of comfort but they never stop to think of how that comfort arrives. It is just like an airbag. An airbag provides safety but that does not mean it is not strong by itself. It is so strong that if it deploys in a certain way it can kill the one it's supposed to protect just like a seat belt has been known to damage the collar bone of those it is designed to protect.

Peace is a cushion but it has strength. The difference with the airbag and seat belt is that peace will not hurt the one it is protecting. It hurts the one who wants to hurt the one it protects. When one has this peace, it is evident they are fathered by God. In fact this is the fastest way to see if one is saved, when they have peace about them. You see, this shows that they will be victors and conquerors!

Those With Peace Are More Than Conquerors

You are more than a conqueror as a peacemaker. You are born to win and to control circumstances but not to go under them.

Blessed are the peacemakers: for they shall be called the children of God.

Matthew 5:8-10

I mentioned earlier that if you ask people how they are feeling they normally answer, "I am doing well under the circumstances", and I always answer, "What are you doing UNDER the circumstances?" A believer does not need to be under the circumstances! We are born of the Almighty God! In fact the Bible goes further than just calling us conquerors. It says;

"...we are more than conquerors..."

Romans 8:37

You see a conqueror is lower in stature in comparison to 'more than conqueror'. When someone is 'more than a conqueror' it signifies resting. We are no longer fighting. If one is more than a conqueror; they have won the battle. They are resting.

They are past conquering. We are no longer in a battle; we have won the battle and are resting peacefully!

That is being more than a conqueror. That does not mean there are no longer wars. It simply means wars might still be declared by your opponents, bad circumstances might still be coming your way but you have found a way that will make you fly over wars. You have peace. You have an army around your heart. You are hemmed in.

No wonder the word says;

"...no weapon formed (fashioned) against me shall prosper..."

Isaiah 54:17

Notice the scripture. Weapons are going to be formed against you and I, but they will not prosper. Their effects will not be felt. That's a blessing of the Lord. See, love is the secret, but understanding how to fully love through the revelation of love's components makes you a master in life. It makes you have joy. It makes you remove hate from your life. You see, why hate when you can love? Why hate when you have peace that can strengthen your joy? Why hate when there a sentinel posted around your heart.

Live in peace and walk in peace. Throw your problems to Jesus, for he knows how to deal with them.

When police knock at your door with summons, send the army guarding your heart you will see what happens. When the doctor speaks to you about that sickness, let the ears of your soldiers who guard your heart listen instead of you and you will see what will happen to that report. When doubts and fear knock on the door of your heart, send Jesus to answer them. The soldiers mounting the door of your heart will answer. When the bailiffs knock at your door, send the garrison on your heart to answer. Let every problem that knocks at your door be met by the army that hems you in. Let the cushioning peace you have answer them. I assure you this peace will know what to say and how to respond. It is very simple. Do you see that?

After that you need to move to other areas of the fruit and see the six areas that will make your joy full. Stay with this revelation here and see the miracles that it will bring. You can enjoy your life today, it is possible!

CHAPTER FOUR

Take A Hold Of Longsuffering

For joy to work with peace there is a part that you need to adopt in order to enjoy life NOW. This part towards having full joy is called longsuffering.

I understand that some would say, 'what is longsuffering?' This part of the fruit is more difficult to understand than the rest. Many believers when they see the word Longsuffering they get all spiritual and confuse themselves, so even if they want joy, it cannot be full. They take longsuffering to mean suffering for a long time.

Longsuffering does not mean to suffer long. It is not an instruction from the Lord to suffer. This is a recipe to finding great joy and yes full joy. It has nothing to do with suffering long. It has nothing to do with painful episodes becoming part of one's life.

Let's see Apostle Paul again in Galatians 5:22

"The fruit of the spirit is love... longsuffering..."

Notice Longsuffering is taken from the word "Makrothumia". This Greek word is made up of two words "thumia" and "makro". The first word thumia is translated as heat, hot or sometimes in reference to fire. It is a burning substance. This is exactly where we got the word thermal from. The word makro is a preposition, which is an intensification of that fire. Makrothumia is intensified fire that comes out of the believer. The translators of the bible translates it as long suffering when in actual fact long suffering as we know it today has little to do with even enduring. It has nothing to do with suffering long.

The Partnership

Notice that for joy to be full, it needs longsuffering and that longsuffering has to partner with other parts of the fruit of the spirit in order for believers to be full of joy. Full joy is possible. It is very achievable but in order to achieve it, one must have the ability to adopt intensified fire. Joy calls for this fire never to stop. It siphons power from this Makrothumia. Do you see the continued interlink of all this. It's inter-twinned to such an extent that if one part of the fruit is ignored or not taken in to consideration all the others will not work properly. Joy will not work properly so you will keep saying you have joy when you actually have happiness.

Let's look at what this Longsuffering is all about!

This Longsuffering

The word makrothumia is not just endurance; it is an ability one adopts that says no matter what happens to me I will never lose the fire burning in me to go forward. This is the part that gives joy its fire, the fire to never let your fire die. You see Makrothumia is like patience, Longsuffering is also referred to as patience. Patience is being mild, gentle, and constant in all circumstances. Like makrothumia, the real test of patience is not in waiting, but in how one acts while he or she is waiting. Notice makrothumia or longsuffering does not concentrate on the problem or outdoing it, but concentrates on adding the fire to such an extent that when life throws punches that may quench the fire in you, it is constantly adding fire to your life that you will never know that the fire in your life was about to go out. It is a continuous flowing of fire. It is not concentrating on pain as such but on adding fire to joy but this it does through the control of the soul.

I recently read about a man of God who was arrested more than a hundred times in one year simply because the authorities did not approve of his healing crusades. He was not fazed by this, he kept organising crusades and people were continuously blessed.

A person who has developed makrothumia will be able to put up with things without losing his or her temper. It is like patience and yes in it is patience.

It contains patience. Scripture tells us;

"But let patience have her perfect work, that ye may be perfect and entire, wanting (lacking) nothing."

James 1:4

Reaching this point of fire continuously flowing out of you is categorically a process which takes a lot of practice. Longsuffering involves your soul which contains mind, will and emotions so it has to be done out of one's choice. One ought to choose to do the things that catapult them to a higher degree where the fire to do anything becomes resident in them. So you see that this longsuffering involves a different endurance since it contains patience but surely is not limited to enduring. It has a different type of endurance that causes your fire to become sizzling hot when you are challenged by circumstances. So instead of the circumstances causing the fire to go out, the Makrothumia or longsuffering, creates a counter balance and gives more fire than the previous one. It adds a lot more fire, more than what was there before the circumstances were experienced. That is why you see the scripture that says;

"...when the enemy comes like a flood, the Spirit of God shall RAISE a standard..."

Isaiah 59:19

Do you see that? The standard is raised so the fire keeps burning. When the enemy comes the Holy

Spirit raises the standard. You see the fire that God has to counter the devil. When you adopt this fire by the Holy Spirit and yes you are a believer so you have the Holy Spirit, you are able to outsmart the devil. That means the more he attacks, the more you are able to have more fire to such an extent that you will be too expensive for the devil to mess with.

To prove what I just said, see this scripture;

"...if the thief be found he shall repay sevenfold..."

Proverbs 6:30-31

With makrothumia from the Holy Spirit, which is activated through choice in the mind in your soul, you become expensive for the devil to attack. You see every time he attacks he would need to repay sevenfold. Do you see how longsuffering helps the believer? Do you see how it gives the believer the fire for their joy? It is a great part towards having full joy that will get the believer's fire not to be quenched and it is very easy to achieve because it requires your will power.

Some people get quenched when problems come. They have not practised to keep ticking when they hit a snag. They have no ability to keep the fire going. They have no thumia in them. What they have is intensified fear that robs you of joy. So the believer without fail ought to have makrothumia, intensified hot fire. The believer should carry in them a great fire power to add on to their lives when the devil is hunting them down.

A Point To Note

Notice again that we have just finished the first group of the fruit of the spirit. The first group contains those parts which turn one's thought toward God. Joy, for we rejoice in the Lord and Peace from God that surpasses all understanding. This is all towards God so it occurs in the Spirit.

In the second group that is where we find longsuffering, and the parts that direct our attention to our soul, that is the mind, will and emotions. These deal with how we interact with ourselves. Kindness, Goodness and Longsuffering are in this group that relates to our soul. It deals with our contact with the mind, will and emotions.

The third group of parts refer more directly to the control of the fruit over our body. It relates to you personally. This group consists of Faithfulness Gentleness, Meekness and Self-control, all which help joy to be full.

Now in dealing with Longsuffering as mentioned before the word for Longsuffering is Makrothumia which has nothing to do with suffering long. It does not focus on endurance though it involves it. Makrothumia is not just endurance; it is an ability never to let your fire die. You see Makrothumia is like patience, Longsuffering is also referred to as patience. Patience is being mild, gentle, and constant in all circumstances. Like makrothumia, the real test of patience is not in waiting, but in how one acts while he or she is waiting. It focuses on not losing fire by adding an ever flowing fire power that paralyses every hard situation the believer may face.

It is also good to deal with the word patience since we have found out that it is inside makrothumia. In other words there is no makrothumia which does not contain patience. Patience is the Greek word "hupomone" which is a compound word made up of two other words: "hupo" which is a preposition meaning 'under' and "moneo" which is a verb meaning to 'remain' or 'abide'. Thus, the idea is to 'remain under' or 'abide under' difficult circumstances - as when it is not possible to escape or avoid them. This as you see bears real resemblance to makrothumia because hupomone is inside makrothumia.

The KJV translates the word as longsuffering, and patient. The basic idea is twofold. Objectively, we show longsuffering, and subjectively we exercise patience. The main idea is that longsuffering is the ability to endure everything that is necessary to reach a desired goal. Look at few other verses that use this word.

If you look again at the meaning of Longsuffering and the two words in Greek which describe it you will see a striking resemblance. Makrothumia is from a compound word made up of the word "macros" which also means 'long' or 'far' and "thumos" which is 'wrath' or 'fierceness'. Although thumos can mean wrath or fierceness, its usage in this compound form carries the idea of 'temper.'

So it means long wrath or long fierceness which proves the point we have made before that this has little to do with suffering long. In fact it is something stemming from the believer.

The fire is not coming towards the believer. It is coming from the believer, right from the Spirit and controlling the soul by choice. The believer then is a fire house throwing out fire, throwing out long wrath or long fierceness. This is by no means being short tempered; it is dealing with the devil and his circumstances seeing fire being produced by you and him running away from the fire. It gives a picture of the devil holding a hose pipe of problems trying to quench your fire for God and for life but would not get to you because even where he is standing the fire from you is reaching him constantly so he is burning constantly. When he adds more water to quench the fire he sees that your makrothumia increases seven times more than the water of problems and hardships he throws at you. This is makrothumia. A power that shows more fire in problems and outside of problems, your fire will still be shooting out.

Thus, makrothumia denotes remaining in a state of emotional quietness in the face of unfavourable circumstances, remaining in a state of fire in my mind so as to push joy up and also remaining in a state of quietness in my will to remain fired up and increasing my fire in the presence of my enemies.

There are definitions for longsuffering and patience and some of these are; to be of a long spirit, not to lose heart, to persevere patiently and bravely in enduring misfortunes and troubles; to be mild and slow in avenging; to be longsuffering, to be slow to anger, to be slow to punish.

As one can see, these words are very close in meaning and it is impossible to make a hard and fast distinction between where one or the other might be used to denote the idea of endurance and patience. Within the context of Colossians 1:11, the word translated by patience emphasizes endurance in the midst of difficult circumstances whereas the word translated by longsuffering emphasizes the attitude or frame of mind we are to have during the difficult time.

A person who has developed patience will be able to put up with things without losing his or her temper. Longsuffering involves not losing temper because if you lose your temper you will lose your fire. So a believer has to make the choice by God not to lose temper and to mount the ability to be slow to anger.

Slow To Anger

Let's we look at the word longsuffering from the Hebrew word "erakhap", which is a combination of two words, the word slow and the word anger. One needs to be slow to anger for there to be fire flowing continuously out of you as a believer.

I was like that before. I would lose my temper at a whim and realised that when I lost my temper it was difficult for my will to push me towards achieving my goals. I would try to go back to my work but I would fail until I got back my composure. In other words this slowed my progress down.

Full joy is seen when one is longsuffering and by that longsuffering they are slow to anger.

Being slow to anger helps your joy to be full. Don't be moved. The word says:

"...Love is...slow to anger..."

Do you see that love comes back again? It is all because joy is part of the fruit called love as aforementioned and so being slow to anger will help joy. It is a great chain of a process. It is a great thing when you know that longsuffering pushes you high up towards your goals and as a result your joy becomes full. Now you will be noticing the results of your joy focussing on the Lord. Be a person who is willing to put your anger out and locked. This nature though pushed by the soul is also closely related to God like all the parts of the fruit.

Living like God

You see these principles in this book are really characteristics of God. The word says:

"...as he is so are we..."

1 john 4:17

As God is so are we. We have these characteristics in us because God made us like he is. Because what God is saying about His longsuffering is that He is slow to anger. He is slow to exercise His wrath. He is slow to practice his fierceness. So longsuffering brings to mind tolerance. Long suffering speaks about tolerance. The bible says that part of the glory of God is His tolerance towards all the wrongs that we do, not because he loves the wrongs, but because he is very slow to anger. He does not want to get angry too quick towards us. It's his character. We also have to be slow to anger just like God.

God has marvellous longsuffering. His fire is continuously flowing. He has great patience no wonder for years the world has not just crawled into oblivion. It did not burst.

Watch some few scriptures about the Lord's character which should be reflected on us as well through our soul.

Romans 2:4 Or do you show contempt for the riches of his kindness, tolerance and patience, not realizing that God's kindness leads you toward repentance? (NIV)

Hebrews 6:12 We do not want you to become lazy, but to imitate those who through faith and patience inherit what has been promised. (NIV)

Galatians 5:22 But the fruit of the Spirit is love, joy, peace, patience, kindness, goodness …. (NIV)

See Longsuffering in God's character;

Exodus 34:6 And the LORD passed by before him, and proclaimed, The LORD, The LORD God, merciful and gracious, longsuffering, and abundant in goodness and truth,

Numbers 14:18 The LORD is longsuffering, and of great mercy, forgiving iniquity and transgression, and by no means clearing the guilty, visiting the iniquity of the fathers upon the children unto the third and fourth generation.

Psalms 86:15 But thou, O Lord, art a God full of compassion, and gracious, longsuffering, and plenteous in mercy and truth.

See the same longsuffering in Salvation:

2 Peter 3:15 And account that the longsuffering of our Lord is salvation; even as our beloved brother Paul also according to the wisdom given unto him hath written unto you;

This longsuffering is also seen through Christ's intercession for the believer and is also experienced by us. This longsuffering also leads to repentance. See it here that when the Lord shows longsuffering he expects something to happen after that. He wants us to answer back in a certain way. Longsuffering should lead to repentance so is you too exercise it, it will lead into your problems bowing down to you.

Look at these scriptures;

Romans 2:4 Or despisest thou the riches of his goodness and forbearance and longsuffering; not knowing that the goodness of God leadeth thee to repentance?

2 Peter 3:9 The Lord is not slack concerning his promise, as some men count slackness; but is longsuffering to us-ward, not willing that any should perish, but that all should come to repentance.

Look at the expectation that the Lord has when he practises longsuffering. Note also that he does this continuously. It is not done by him sometimes and forgets it the next. No, God is always longsuffering because he knows the rewards of it. It encourages repentance.

Joel 2:13 And rend your heart, and not your garments, and turn unto the LORD your God: for he is gracious and merciful, slow to anger, and of great kindness, and repenteth him of the evil.

The Lord also exhibited this longsuffering in forgiving sins.

Romans 3:25 Whom God hath set forth to be a propitiation through faith in his blood, to declare his righteousness for the remission of sins that are past, through the forbearance of God;

God does not just talk about longsuffering; He has already proven that he can do it so we are left with no excuse for not practising longsuffering. This is pure encouragement. Remember the scripture in Romans 2 vs. 21,22;

"...you that preach a man should not steal, do you steal? You that say a man should not commit adultery, do you commit adultery? you that abhor idols, do you commit

sacrilege"

This scripture says if you command others to do something, you yourself should demonstrate that you can do that also. You should demonstrate you can be longsuffering too. God did it; he does not only command it but shows that he can do it too. He did it for his people.

Note;

Isaiah 30:18 And therefore will the LORD wait, that he may be gracious unto you, and therefore will he be exalted, that he may have mercy upon you: for the LORD is a God of judgment: blessed are all they that wait for him.

Ezekiel 20:17 Nevertheless mine eye spared them from destroying them; neither did I make an end of them in the wilderness.

He did it towards the wicked;

Romans 9:22 What if God, willing to shew his wrath, and to make his power known, endured with much longsuffering the vessels of wrath fitted to destruction:

1 Peter 3:20 Which sometime were disobedient, when once the longsuffering of God waited in the days of Noah, while the ark was a preparing, wherein few, that is, eight souls were saved by

He practised longsuffering towards Jerusalem;

Matthew 23:37 O Jerusalem, Jerusalem, thou

that killest the prophets, and stonest them which are sent unto thee, how often would I have gathered thy children together, even as a hen gathereth her chickens under her wings, and ye would not!

He practised it towards Paul;

1 Timothy 1:16 Howbeit for this cause I obtained mercy, that in me first Jesus Christ might shew forth all longsuffering, for a pattern to them which should hereafter believe on him to life everlasting.

God's longsuffering is the one he imparted in us meaning we have the same ability and will power to practice longsuffering just like God has. That is a bonus that helps our joy to be full. It makes peace intact and boosts our joy. This same power is the one that God uses and employs to endure everything that is necessary to accomplish all that he has planned. When you adopt it you will be endowed by the power to accomplish your goals in the earth and everywhere else.

You and I cannot always control our emotions and therefore often fail in an intended purpose, so we need to have longsuffering so that our will will take a hold of our emotions in the soul through the spirit, and bring them in to subjection. God never, in any sense, loses control of himself. We get mad and throw up our hands and say, "I don't need this or that problem", but God is calm with peace and fire not to stop by long suffering's ability to spit continuous fire.

I met a lady once whose emotions were all over

the place. One minute she would be mad wanting to fight anyone who happened to cross her path with the smallest of offences. She was ever ready to fight. The next minute she would be weeping like a baby overcome with emotion triggered by the smallest thing. This emotional rollercoaster cost her lots of things in life.

A believer, like God should never lose his cool! That is why every purpose of God will surely succeed.

A lack of longsuffering is manifested by ascribing to others bad motives when we may have misinterpreted actions or words. A lack of longsuffering is shown when we have a short fuse that causes us to say and do things in retaliation to others. The Hebrew writer says;

"For ye have need of patience, that, after ye have done the will of God, ye might receive the promise."

Hebrews 10:36

This verse in Hebrews proves to us that we may lose our miracles and even joy through lack of longsuffering. Lack of makrothumia which contains hupomone will cripple your chance to get a life full of joy. This implies that we can lose the promise by impatience.

Longsuffering Sees The Miracle

Longsuffering is said to be a fruit of the Spirit, that is, it is the result of having the teaching of the Spirit in one's heart. In this context Paul admonishes;

Galatians 5:25 says,
"If we live in the Spirit, let us also walk in the Spirit."

That is, live the life dictated by the Spirit, absorbing His qualities into your soul and making a decision to get that life of longsuffering to take over your world. That is the life where miracles take place. As a believer we should never lose our cool. We should be cool and slow to anger. Circumstance should never anger us. I have adopted that life and it shows through when I walk and when I talk. My life is possessed with happiness. It is a life of composure that my enemies cannot gain entry. Joy is full when you see the best happening.

Longsuffering has to help with a lot of things. It controls your life. It gets you to a level of joy that your enemies and the devil himself will not understand. The fire it produces burns the devil and cripples all the problems. Your enemies themselves will see your state of composure as you choose to forgive them.
Paul said in Romans 14:1;

"Him that is weak in the faith receive ye, but not to doubtful disputations."

And in Romans 15:1, He says;

"We then that are strong ought to bear the infirmities of the weak, and not to please ourselves."

Other Avenues To Achieving Longsuffering

How to handle these involves soaking yourself into scriptures that talk about God's longsuffering because in seeing how God's attitude towards you works you can walk into how you can forgive those who wrong you. Your attitude determines the outcome that influences your joy. Enjoying life now starts when longsuffering is coupled with peace and also other parts of the fruit of the Spirit.

It is also advisable to break fellowship with people that cause this to happen on a daily basis. There are some people who are always negative and everything they do is based upon fear that things might not come to pass. It is in this that people of God need to be careful not to shun people but avoid arguments whilst maintaining our love for our fellow brother. This is a great aid in enjoying life, when one chooses a life of no arguments, a life of solitude with regards to arguments but a life of fellowship that only gives life. Be a life giver and burn with an ever ending fire towards life. Don't let people quench your fire and this is done through breaking fellowship with negative people.

Now the best way is calmness and having an, "I can do", attitude towards life. Notice that since God's will, again, is that Christ may be formed in each of us. Trials and testing seem to be the way this longsuffering is accomplished when we remain calm in their face. See that God Himself wants us conformed into His image so that others may see Christ in us and truly want what we have. When we genuinely reflect Christ in all that we do, others will come to the conclusion that will reflect Jesus and so our problems are paralysed by us looking like Christ. The devil himself will fear. Your problems will disintegrate and your joy will be aided.

You find great longsuffering through strength gained in times of trial, by waiting calmly and in silence, yet with determination and will to move on every minute and second of life. You see impatience does not work. Reacting to every problem and every hardship with anger or immaturity only serves to achieve temporary changes that just as quickly as they are received they are lost. It leads to having a temporary solution to a permanent problem which will only serve to postpone your problem. Longsuffering is a permanent solution to a permanent enemy called the devil. With Longsuffering you will have set yourself to a life of defeating the purpose of the devil over your life.

Longsuffering will keep you burning. This is the reality of longsuffering over your life. So be steadfast in your waiting and hold on to your integrity. Don't lose your integrity. Keep your composure as you add fire to your life. Spit fire. Cause fire to come out constantly, in days of happiness and even in the day of trouble.

However, since this longsuffering is in the group that takes charge of the soul other avenues of making makrothumia to work in your journey towards joy is to employ the other parts that control the soul. These are goodness and longsuffering.

CHAPTER FIVE

Be Kind

We have often talked about kindness and the word has become 'watered' it does not carry as much as it should. Kindness is the noun form of **kind** which means being of a friendly or generous nature; showing sympathy, mercy, empathy, or understanding; beneficial to something's function.

The Greek word used in Galatians 5:22 is *"chrestotes"*. It is a form of the Greek word "chrestos". Its main meaning is "useful, fit for use", but it has copied meanings of "useful for others" but stems from the will hence its control of the soul. In the Septuagint which is the oldest translation of the Hebrew Scriptures (Old Testament) into Greek, it shows a very deep meaning of the word chrestotes. In this it is used in connection to gemstones to describe their value.

There is something you need to know here, the

Hebrew word for kindness usually implies a more vigorous sort of mercy than kindness usually bears in English. A related Greek term is "eleos" which often translates the Hebrew, "chesed" in the Septuagint, is a violent sort of kindness. It relates to your spirit getting a hold of your mind and pushing it to kill your flesh and sterilise your will in your soul in to a state where it would be kind.

This is the violent act of your spirit over the soul to control it into a level where it becomes a servant and by that act produces kindness.

You see that many ways that promote joy here under the fruit of the spirit do not bring out the very best they should bring if taken at face value. One needs to get deeper with the Lord to know how to enjoy life now. Kindness here at face value denotes a passive way of doing things. A certain weakness that causes submission is also regarded as kindness if the definition is not defined well.

This is the power that released the power to heal the sick when the Lord Jesus did it. He was a man full of kindness that when he reached the sick or when the sick met with him something in him would spin inside and cause the power of God to be released. This thing was kindness. Look at this:

"..He was moved by compassion..."

Mark 1:41

You see compassion contains kindness. First he would have kindness upon them and then by this mercy he would spring into healing them He was moved inside by kindness. Mercy would get a hold of him and he would perform miracles. At one meeting kindness in him caused him to multiply food in order to feed more than five thousand people. He said:

"...We should not let these people go to their houses hungry..."

When you look at this you would be mistaken to think all he did was being kind but you see his kindness towards the people and within him caused the power of God to be released so he could perform one of the most celebrated miracles in the Bible. He changed two fish and five loaves of bread into lunch that could feed more than five thousand.

Kindness was the switch to power. It was the detonator to the power locked inside the Lord. This is what will also happen in your journey to joy. Kindness to self and to other causes you to be a person of power. It causes you to be an overflowing stream of power. It is something that will get you to get be known in your world as a person of power. You will be known as a person that cannot easily be moved. This was the life of Jesus Christ our Lord. He was so kind that instead of people seeing weakness, they were seeing a man full of virtue. Notice that your power for greatness can be switched on by kindness and your joy moved to another degree because you are a kind person that paralyses even your enemies.

When people gossip about you and you keep calm

because you are kind to the wrongs they did to you. You remain peaceful because you are kind. You become a person who is longsuffering because you are kind. Do you still see the interlink?

If kindness in you is practised you will have life.

See **Proverbs 21:21**

"Whoever pursues righteousness and kindness will find life, righteousness, and honour."

Job 6:14 says;

"He who withholds kindness from a friend forsakes the fear of the Almighty."

Some people are born selfish. In our earliest days we beg to be served and provided for. We love kindness when it is bestowed upon us. It is all about me, me, and me! The question might arise in our mind; Why should I do her chores or why should I be patient and listen to him? They won't return the kindness! It won't do me any good!

Does it need to benefit us before we commit a kindness? It is a requirement of God to love kindness and exercise it humbly and cheerfully, Micah 6:8.

The Bible, however, tells us about a successful heart transplant which Ezekiel saw. He saw kindness being implanted into us because as Romans 5:5 says;

"...The love of God was shed abroad in our hearts..."

See kindness is already in you because love was put in you, in fact shed all over your heart when you received the Lord. So all you really need is to practice it and get the benefits of joy that the Lord promises. Let's notice what the prophet Ezekiel saw concerning this heart transplant:

"...I will give you a new heart and put a new spirit in you; I will remove from you your heart of stone and give you a heart of flesh..." (Ezekiel 36:26).

Jesus Christ our Lord showed this kindness when He was kind to the sinning woman who anointed His feet.

Kindness As Your Response

Kindness is your response to the challenge if you are led by the Spirit. Now you have taken the fifth step. The fourth step you are being challenged. The fifth step if you are led by the Spirit you will not respond an eye for an eye, a tooth for a tooth, a leg for a leg. If you respond by taking revenge, you just show people that you are not led by the Spirit. See how important the fruit of the Spirit is. If you respond in any other way, it becomes the work of the flesh.

Notice that violence is mentioned there in verse 19 and 20;

The works of the flesh are evident, which are

adultery, fornication, uncleanness, lewdness, idolatry, sorcery, hatred, contentions, jealousies, and outbursts of wrath, selfish ambitions, dissensions, heresies, envy, murders, drunkenness, revelries and the like.

If you are led by the Spirit you will show kindness in responding to any challenges. You repay evil with good. That may cut off a lot of people's so called leading.

CHAPTER SIX

Goodness

Goodness is the state or quality of being good, especially morally good or beneficial. In a sense, it's the quality of having quality. Other words used in describing goodness are beneficial, gainful, useful, helpful, profitable, and excellent. Moral "goodness" is grouped with words such as uprightness, virtue, benevolence, worth, value and generosity. We just need more 'good' people in this world, I'm sure you agree. So I'd like to dig a little deeper and show you the revelation behind goodness and how it relates to enjoying your life more.

The Greek term in Galatians 5 is "agathosune", which is from agathos meaning good-natured, helpful and beneficial. Another form of agathos is found together with pistos in the phrase "good and faithful" servants, in the parable of the talents.

Goodness Starts By The Knowledge Of God

Goodness carries the strings of knowledge. It is something that works together with God's knowledge but does a little bit more than just carrying knowledge. One who wants goodness has to understand God's word so he or she has to have knowledge in God and with God. You see God knows that Knowledge puffs up. See what I Corinthians 8:1 says;

"...Knowledge puffs up..."

Knowledge in a life of a person who is not good can bring about pompousness. Even a little knowledge will cause one to be pompous. However, goodness will hold such a display in check and guide knowledge to build up rather than destroy.

I have seen some people who became like fools when they managed to memorise two or three scriptures. These people will be quoting scripture every time like the Bible is going out of fashion. They will spew out scriptures even if they were not asked. You see there is nothing wrong in quoting scripture but something is very wrong when this is done foolishly. Knowledge sure puffs up. Many people like this will be religious to the extent that the knowledge they want to display is not in their lives but they think they can just show people their ability. However that display can be, not always, a display of immaturity and also a display of lack of goodness.

Goodness carries knowledge first before it goes

to other areas and when one shows the above behaviour and yet their lives do not reflect what they are trying to show then there is lack of goodness. This is the beginning of goodness. It starts with the knowledge of God being in one's life.

Goodness Versus Kindness

When you look in the New Testament these two seem to be very similar but when you look closely at the Hebrew and Greek uses you see something way different. Hebrew, like in English, with regards to these words, has a broader application.

The Greek word which brings out the 'full flavour' of the word is agathosune (goodness), at first glance will look like it's strikingly similar to chrestotes "kindness". However, deeper examination of its use in the Scriptures reveals a word indicating fanatical activity in doing good. One with goodness here possesses a fanatic approach for goodness. Goodness consumes one that they are now crazy with it. They are 'goodness' crazy. They are consumed with zeal for goodness.

You see, kindness as chrestotes can be seen as is more passive. Kind people seem like they are not violent at all. At first glance they just look very weak until one understands it in a deeper way then they see the command that causes one to be a fanatic. You see for joy to consume you, you need to be fanatic to doing acts of goodness. You need to be good with the zeal evident. Zeal to do good should consume you. It should get you to a level of practicing kindness to the extent where people see you as a man or woman of goodness and you come across to everyone as a kind person. This is a violent act but a positive act. It is an act that is very forward and direct. It carries a punch to it just like we saw in kindness.

The Big Difference

What is the difference? *Agathosune(goodness)* might, and could, rebuke and discipline; chrestotes(kindness) can only help. The lord Jesus showed agathosune when He cleansed the Temple and drove out those who were making it a bazaar; but He showed chrestotes when He was kind to the sinning woman who anointed His feet. The Christian needs that goodness which at the same time can be kind and strong. Know where to be strong!

That is the word says in Matthew 10 vs. 16:

"...be as wise as a serpent and as peaceful as a dove..."

The understanding of kindness and its relationship to goodness will cause you to know what to do at different times in your life. It shows you when to react strong and when to react in a passive like manner. This helps your joy because if you react with kindness where you need to use goodness you will without fail cause problems to your life. This is the sense here. Joy is aided when you as a believer know when to use what to use with regards to different situations in your life.

Agathosune is therefore an active way of doing things. In fact it can be taken as an aggressive goodness. It is more than an excellence of character; it is character energized, expressing itself in active good. It is a bubbly character. An explosive character that people cannot ignore. It is a character that confuses the enemy. This is what Jeremiah had in chapter 20 when he said:

"...my enemies will suffer everlasting confusion..."

That is the kind of confusion your enemies and any problem you face will get because goodness in you will cause renewed energy to churn out of you. Your enemies will see the fire coming out of you.

Agathosune is goodness, but it does not spare rebuke to produce good in others. Thus God can correct, sometimes very severely, and it is goodness in action. In fact the bible says in the book of Hebrews 12 vs. 6

"...For whom the Lord loveth he chasteneth, and scourgeth every son whom he receiveth..."

Thus parents can correct their child, and it is good because it helps produce a responsible adult. I know a number of parents who will not lay a hand on their children no matter how wild they become because it's a "different world with different methods". Yet the word of God here is saying every child he receives he scourges. He only disciplines those He loves. That is goodness. So learn to know when goodness is to be applied and when kindness is to be applied as well. Be balanced.

Three Kinds Of Goodness

Goodness is also much related to purity in the person. Purity and goodness have a close link that one cannot be good unless they are pure. There is no way one can claim they are good unless they are pure. This is a big one because I know some of you will be thinking; now this purity is very hard to do but stay with me and let's share the scriptures. There are three levels/kinds of goodness that I would like to share with you so you need to stay with this thought.

The First Kind Of Goodness

There are three Greek words for purity. Now don't get too caught up with the Greek I just need to go back to the original sense of the word as this is where the revelation lies. The first one here I want to deal with is 'Katharos', which means to be cleansed or washed. It carries the same meaning like our English word pure. It's an undefiled purity with no speck of impurity whatsoever. It is used as in a pure heart or a clean heart. This is the beginning of purity, the purity of the heart. You see there is also the purity of the soul and that of the body, believe it or not. Katharos talks of the purity of the heart. **It is the same Greek word that Jesus used in John 15: 3**

"You are already katharos (cleansed or washed) because of the Word which I have spoken to you."

You are already clean. The Lord Jesus here knows that He is talking about believers so he uses the word katharos and says you are already katharos meaning to say there is nothing here you can do to be katharos (cleansed) unless he katharoses you himself! Do you get it? As a Christian he has already katharosed you through his word when he saved you. Jesus spent three years cleaning them up by teaching them. So the only thing we need to do is learn from His word because it is katharosing us every time we read it. We become good. We become pure.

The teaching of the Lord makes us good by making us pure in our hearts. It removes us from adhering to the wrong things. If then we want to be good, we would need purity of the heart. Christ is the word and The Word teaching us His word will katharos us so we can be good! Remember what the Lord said. Let's see that again;

Jesus said;

"You are katharos (good) because of the Word that I have spoken onto you."

The Second Kind Of Goodness

The other word here for goodness or purity is *'eilikrines'*. Now the word *'eilikrines'* is a totally different word and it also mean pure, transparent which is in a way a sign of great goodness. This word is a combination of two words which are *'eili'* and *'krines'*. The first word *'krines'* means referee. The word *'eili'* has its roots in the word glow. That means the word *'eilikrines'* means the purity which comes when the referee proves its glow. It shines and its shining is proven by a referee. The referee validates its light that is the sense it brings. So God has to approve you by judging you or being an umpire to your soul. You see when something is brought to a shining light and the bright light exposes it, its purity is exposed. Its purity comes to the surface. That means your mind has to be exposed to God's grade of judgement for it to shine well enough.

The Third Kind Of Goodness

When Apostle Paul was asking us to be sincere in the book of Corinthians he was actually asking us to be good. The word sincere here is the same as the word simplicity as shown in the word. Haplotes is the word simplicity and is closely linked to sincere here. So Apostle Paul was admonishing us to be good with a mind that this would increase our joy. This was Apostle Paul's ultimate goal, the joy of the believer. Look at the scripture below as we start with this word sincere then we move on to haplotes when we've describe simplicity:

1 Cor.5: 8 *"Therefore let us keep the feast, not with old leaven, nor with the leaven of malice and wickedness, but with the*

unleavened bread of sincerity and truth."

When you see the word 'leaven' you know we are talking about being bad. Yeasts can be found everywhere in nature, especially on plants and fruits. After fruits fall off the tree, fruits become rotten through the activity of moulds, which form alcohol and carbon dioxide from the sugars in it. Sometimes drunk animals appear in the news because they have eaten these spoiled fruits. Funny, but true. So yeast is bad according to the word here. It carries rotten components so Apostle Paul says:

1 Cor.5: 8 *"Therefore let us keep the feast, not with old leaven, nor with the leaven of malice and wickedness, but with the unleavened bread of sincerity and truth."*

So the above verse shows us that Apostle Paul is talking about purity because leaven in the bread defiles it. Remember this is the same thing the Lord Jesus Himself told his disciples in Matthew 16 vs. 16, He says:

"...beware of the leaven of the Pharisees..."

Here he was telling them to run away from being defiled. The Lord wanted his disciples to keep goodness that will not be defiled .Jesus was telling them to be sincere, to be pure, and to be upright. So when you want joy to be in you, you ought to become sincere. That is what you do. You become an upright person. God is faithful; He will apply that joy unspeakable today as long as you reach out to Him.

But what is a sincere person? A sincere person is mainly seen by what comes out of their mouth. A sincere person is a simple person in the sense of simplicity. Notice that the Pharisees would speak volumes and the Lord told His disciples to be aware of what the words were. Did they give a sense of simplicity in the speaker or was there a different feel to their words. Were they saying one thing and doing another? This attitude is seen by the word *haplotes*. In other words he was saying the leaven was their words, in a way telling his own disciples that if they wanted to run away from those words they need to care about what enters into their ears: He was in a way saying;

"...Be careful what you hear..."

What the Pharisees said was the leaven so the sign of a good person is also measured by what comes out of their mouth. A good man is a man of few words. That reminds me of Charles G Finney. He had a minister that volunteered to go and pray for his crusades way before Charles starts preaching. When some people wanted to gossip about this man to Charles G Finney they asked him "what do you think of that minister?" Charles G Finney answered "He is like any man of prayer. He is a man of very few words".

Do you see that? To Finney a man of few words will likely be a man of prayer so prayer also helps to develop this character of a quiet spirit and also this angle of goodness because one becomes a person of few words. The Pharisees on the other hand were people of many words. In a way they were people of the leaven. Their mouths were always open with wrong words coming out yet a believer's goodness is seen by the words in them since they already have another goodness of the heart. See the scripture in Proverbs 4 vs. 23;

"...from the heart are the issues of life..."

Katharos loaded people are people who can have haplotes (sincerity). The heart is good so the mind will also be good if it's controlled by the heart. A good person may not come across as good sometimes but they mean what they say. Their sincerity which here is their goodness will definitely come out. There is no malice in their heart.

However there are people who will always claim to be good. Some will claim to be very sincere but their sincerity is sincerely wrong!

The Pharisees are different. They do one thing and they say another thing. What they say and what they do don't synchronize. They were for the letter and the bible says in 2 Corinthians 3 vs. 6;

"...The letter killeth but the Spirit giveth life..."

Isn't that what the Pharisees are? Jesus says in Matthew 5 vs. 20,

"...unless your righteousness exceeds the righteousness of the Pharisees, you shall

not inherit the kingdom of God..."

In other words he was also saying:

"...unless your goodness exceeds the goodness of the Pharisees, you shall not inherit the kingdom of God..."

You see goodness is not something you just claim you have. It is something with evidence to it. Something that carries proof and people can actually confirm to the fact that you are a good person. Good people are contagious. You sit around them long enough they will either bore you to death or push you into being good. That is their nature. They are just good and the light in them is very bright so that the darkness in their enemies cannot not stand. It will flee away. These people are full of light.

Notice here how Apostle Paul continues in this light:

In 2 Corinthians we want to look at the different word here in chapter 11: 3

"But I fear, lest somehow, as the serpent deceive Eve by his craftiness, so your minds may be corrupted from the simplicity that is in Christ."

In the scripture above we see another thing which is really in the same league with sincerity the word simplicity is the word 'Haplotes'. Now 'haplotes' has a powerful meaning and it also means a type of transparency and purity. Do you know deceiving and sly people are crafty? They know how to twist and turn their words to deceive. Paul says don't be like that because that is how the serpent is. That is how the devil is. Their yes is not always a yes. You never know when they really mean yes. Because when they yes it might even be a no. So you are never sure with such people. You are never sure. They will not expose the truth. They are not transparent

For example, 2 Cor. 8 vs. 2 says

"That in a great trial of affliction the abundance of their joy and their deep poverty abounded in the riches of their liberality."

The word liberality is the same word 'haplotes' meaning their liberality and the generosity of their spirit that comes forth from their lives. There are no two ways about it here, only what you have deposited inside you is seen in your actions. So their heart is good, their soul is good and now their actions are proving to be good. Now that is what God calls goodness. There is no lying with these guys they are really showing what they have on the inside. When you are good you don't have to swear by anything. You actions will be proof enough. That is why the bible in James 5 vs. 12 says;

"...Don't swear by the earth or by heavens..."

When you are good, your actions will do the swearing on their own. You see I have heard people promise my husband and I heaven on earth in businesses that we run and even in our ever widening ministry. We have seen this proof in many ways. In business I have been promised the earth and people swearing by their pay checks that they were not going to leave us but they did. Many in our churches told pastors that they were now feeling at home in our church that they were not going to go but they did. This swearing did not do them any good because their actions were proving all this wrong. You see their promise could not substitute their bad hearts, bad soul and bad actions. They spoke but they could not act it. Do you see that this goodness is not at all as easy as people think goodness can be explained?

You see that when you are good you don't have to swear by the earth or anything else for that matter. No wonder the word says in Matthew 5 vs. 37,

"...Let your yea be a yea and your no be a no..."

You don't have to swear by anything. If you apply these principles, what you say is what you mean. You mean what you say and say what you mean. That is what you do. That's it. Not trying to make everyone happy by kissing up. What you say is what it is no matter people like it or not. You are a person of your word and your actions. Your 'yes' never means a 'maybe', your yes is yes, your no is no.

You see there are some people who say some things and never leave out the words, "to be honest with you" or "to tell you the truth..." then you know they have been lying all along. This is one of the signs that show you a person has no sincerity. Their words cannot be trusted all the time and they know it that is why they want you to know that this time they are being honest with you. Some say "God is my witness..." you know they might be telling you the truth at that time but that shows they do not always tell the truth. Something is very bad in them that they need to put the word God in front for them to show people that they are truthful or to validate a point. This is a sign of lack of goodness of the heart, goodness of the souls and also a lack of goodness of the actions.

You are a transparent person. With you there is no hiding. You hide nothing from people. You have great integrity and every genuine person would want you close by. Even bad people would want to do business with you.

How To Flow In Goodness

You see here that goodness is in threefold. There is goodness of the heart which is related to *katharos*. There is goodness of the soul which is related to the word eilikrines. And there is goodness in your action, which is *haplotes*. One then cannot claim that they are really good until they are good in three areas. First in their hearts, then in their souls and ultimately in their actions or in their body. Goodness therefore is not a matter of talking, it is a 'violent' goodness that causes one to be called good and stems from way in the spirit and then in the soul and as aforementioned in the actions of the person. This is the way it is.

CHAPTER SEVEN

Be Filled With Faithfulness

Faithfulness is stick-ability to the prescription. It is sticking to the prescribed order with no reservation and no breaks. Another close look of the word **'faithful'** means loyal, firmly and resolutely sticking with a person, group, cause, belief, or idea and instruction without wavering. Other words describing faithfulness include true, constant, steadfast, devoted, staunch, and trust.

Notice that joy itself when we first dealt with it in chapter one needs one to be devoted to practising principles that promote it. So Faithfulness is a pillar to enjoying life now since one needs to be constant and stick to the prescription of getting to enjoy life now. You see faithfulness hinges on anything that we value as important in our lives combined with commitment. As human beings, we have a powerful tendency to be faithful to what we think is truly important, be it a family name, spouse, friendship, employer, school, athletic team or even certain things like a certain make of car.

To have full joy, 'Faithfulness' is an essential element that each and every Christian must possess. This part of the fruit or pillar for joy is something so important that without it even heaven cannot accept you there. It is one of the things needed if one is to make it to heaven: Just see what the scripture in Revelation 2:10 says;

"Be faithful until death, and I will give you the crown of life"

Do you see that? Without faithfulness, you cannot achieve so many things in life. It is a pillar and one needs to follow. Now the word Faithfulness in the Greek is rendered "pistis." There are 244 uses of the word "pistis" in the King James Version of the New Testament. It primarily means to have a "firm persuasion" which is usually gained from having a conviction based upon hearing and also being unvarying in that conviction.

Developing It

Faithfulness respects the time of the command so to have it one must respect the moment of the command. One must be constant. When God speaks you do what He says there and then not wait and do it later. Let me just give an example here; if you send your son to get you a drink from the refrigerator and your son agrees but goes there after two days what would that be? Though your son finally obeyed by doing what you said, he will have done it too late. In other words he did not respect the time of the command and has shown signs of not being loyal. Even if he had gone after 20 minutes that will be disrespect and that too is not being faithful. So faithfulness sticks to the command and the time it's given in.

This is very easy for a Christian to do since we are children of God. In other words it's our nature to be faithful if we are mature in the Lord. Mature believers are faithful even when they feel they shouldn't be. They are like mango trees they don't need to stand out in the middle of an orchard saying, Now how do I develop mangoes?" A mango tree produces mangoes because that's what mango trees do. And when we are Spirit-led Christians, when we are a branch attached to the vine who is Jesus Christ, then we produce fruit because it's the natural thing to do. We don't have to sit around & think about it and analyze it. But we do have to be careful that our branch is never detached from the vine, or that some disease will destroy our fruitfulness. So there is also a God given ability to emulate His faithfulness. We are faithful because that is also the genetic makeup of our father in heaven. As He is constant, we are to be constant.

In Psalms 37:3 we are told to ***"Trust in the LORD, and do good; dwell in the land and befriend faithfulness."***

There are many people who are following diets down to the letter and succeeding at what they want to achieve. However there are those who can't follow anything to the dot. They struggle with diets or they follow the exercises faithfully but not restrain from over-eating. They will eat like pigs and exercise faithfully so the weight will not shift and they do not get the results they expect. This is not full faithfulness because full faithfulness includes continuing in the tasks that God has given us to complete. To be faithful is to be consistent and reliable in our responsibilities. That is why the word of God says in Luke 16 vs.10

"He that is faithful in that which is least is faithful also in much..."

Be faithful in whatever you do. If it lines up with the word, keep at it no matter how small it is because if you are not faithful enough, God cannot add more to you. If you are to live a life punctuated with joy every step of the way, you need to be faithful enough to follow the principles outlined in the word of God and explained in this book. I have had the privilege of meeting people in our church who you know you can count on for different things. That is being faithful and it is most pleasing in the sight of God.

In life we need to stand for something or we will fall for anything. There is no middle ground. You as a believer in a quest for practicing the joy the Lord put in you should never give up on anything that you set your spirit to do. If you do that would not be faithfulness and ultimately that will remove the pillar for your joy. Don't give up and be committed. The word says in Luke 9 vs. 62

"...any farmer that puts a plough to the ground and looks back is not fit for the harvest..."

You see that joy happens when you do not quit for quitters never win and winners never quit. That is life and as believers we ought to be constant regardless of circumstances;

"...be instant in season and out of season..."

2 Tim 4 vs. 2

That is the word of God encouraging you never to quit. It does not matter what is happening to you. You ought to keep going. Stick to the prescription.

Faithfulness In My Life

When my husband and I first got the push to create a range of hotels around the world called The Angel Valley Hotels it was hard and we got a lot of draw backs. Many said we could not do it. Others were coming with all sorts of nonsense that would have pushed us sideways. We could have easily stopped the dream but faithfulness in us, stick-ability to the prescription made us hang on even in the face of serious opposition.

There was no money, no land to build on and nothing to write home about. There was nothing to start the business with and that is a lot of pain when you have nothing to start the business with but have everything to stop the business pushing you before you even start. It was an uphill struggle in some areas but we remained faithful and it's starting to pay big time. All the people that said we could not do anything are forced now to swallow their doubts and those who still wish it had stopped will still have their hearts broken because joy is in us because of faithfulness. Faithfulness pushed us higher to a level where we are not moved by anything. We stick to the recipe and are loyal to it and also respect the moment of the recipe and the time of it.

We need to seek the Holy Spirit's reinforcement & develop regular, positive, spiritual habits. This world is not a Christian world and we're being pressured on every side to develop negative habits, tempting us to be unfaithful in church attendance, to be unfaithful in prayer, to be unstable in following God, to be unfaithful in sticking to the prescription in the word of God and even in studying the Word of God. We have developed a wishy-washy approach. That is what we have done now. Faithfulness has left our lives. We can no longer be trusted or trust others.

One other area we should be stern in is our financial faithfulness. Faithfulness in money issues is not a very little thing. However, money cannot give eternal life or real meaning in life yet, there is nothing that reveals our spiritual orientation and relationship with God like our attitude toward money. Jesus Christ made it clear that a mark of true spirituality was a right attitude toward wealth. The mark of a godly and righteous man is his preoccupation with God and heavenly treasure.

So when you give you do it constantly and always be on the up in your giving.

Keep going up on your giving. Faithfulness demands improving in whatever you are doing and remaining constant in it. If it's your offerings, faithfulness does not mean just giving a million every Sunday or twenty dollars every Sunday but in increasing your commitment with regards to that. The point with faithfulness is that it is improving your commitment and not just being constant. In all sense if one is constant they will also grow a need to be better at their commitment. You see the ability to be constant if not exercised through God, it will be employed through religious tendencies and this will not be the faithfulness God requires. Faithfulness should be done out of a willing heart that is why it can only be developed through meditation on the word and respecting the time of God's command!

Follow Instructions Don't Try
To Make God Happy

Don't try to make God happy, just follow His instructions. You see we run a problem of trying to make God happy so when God says bring me some wood; we bring him wood already burning just because we assumed he wanted to start a fire when he wanted to create a chair from it. This is a problem of lacking in faithfulness. Understand that God cannot be made happy by your extra services which he did not ask for. Don't try to do God a favour without his permission. If you think this is not on ask Uzzah.

He thought he could help God but that was a mistake. The oxen stumbled and this would cause the Ark of the Covenant to fall. So the guy thought he needed to help and extended his hand and touched the Ark of the Covenant and that is where he died. He tried to do God a favour that God had not approved. That was the problem of Uzzah. He trespassed the anointing.

See 1 Chronicles 13:9-11 says;

"And they came to the threshing floor of Chidon, Uzzah put out his hand to take hold of the ark, for the oxen stumbled. And the anger of the Lord was kindled against Uzzah, and he struck him down because he put out his hand to the ark, and he died there before God. And David was angry because the Lord had broken out against Uzzah. And that place is called Perez-uzza to this day."

Uzzah did not follow instructions. He wanted to help God by doing what God had said should never be done. Faithfulness is not you doing or sticking to what you feel is best but to what God has given you to do. Do not trespass into another person's anointing. It is not recommended. God is not at all overjoyed at people who want to do things that he has said 'no' to just because they feel that is what God wants. For the joy in you to abound, it should be coupled with a heart that says 'I will follow God'. You notice that when you follow God you respect the time of His command otherwise you will be in doubt. Don't ever try to make God happy. God is made glad by those who are loyal to his word and not our tricks in trying to make him happy.

Faith And Faithfulness

Many do not know the difference between faith and faithfulness. Some think faith is another word for faithfulness and the Greek word adds to the confusion. However the difference is also a tricky one and one needs to really understand how the two work. You see, we put our faith in Jesus. We also have to be faithful to Him. When we accept Jesus as Saviour, we put our faith in Him. When we accept Jesus as Lord, we put our faithfulness in Him.

Faithfulness flows out of our framework of faith. Faithfulness is faith revealed. A steadfast focus on who God is and trusting implicitly in His Word enables us to be constant in times of crisis. This type of faithfulness will be a witness to an unbelieving world of the reality of a constant God who never changes.

When we accept salvation, we die that day. We are no longer who we were before. The word of God says we are new creatures and we no longer live for ourselves - we live for Jesus Christ. As believers, we must give our entire life every part of it over to God! And when we do that, we have to be willing to be faithful. Here's what I want you to do; be faithful to do it. It's not a matter of faith; it's a matter of faithfulness.

What is the difference between faith and faithfulness? Can a person have faith without being faithful? Samson gives us the answer to that question. He was a man of tremendous faith.

On one occasion he killed a thousand Philistines with the jaw bone of a donkey (Judges 15:15). At another time he caught three hundred foxes, took them by pairs and tied their tails together with a torch between them, and turned them loose in the wheat fields of the Philistines (Judges 15:4-5). Boy, talk about power! When he left the city of Gaza one night, he ripped off the huge gates from the city wall, and carried them ten miles up a mountain, not down but up the mountain!(Judges 16:1-3). The Philistines couldn't understand how he could do such feats. Samson was not a huge, muscular man. He didn't look any different to any other man hence the Philistines quest to find out what it was that gave him strength. Where did he get such strength? He had great faith. He believed, and the Holy Spirit anointed him to do things that were otherwise humanly impossible.

But Samson had a weakness. He was not faithful. God had instructed him not to marry anyone that was not from his own country, he didn't listen to God. Faithfulness should have told him to stick to the prescription God had already given him. He had faith, but he was not faithful.

So faithfulness as said before deals with what we do and how constant we are as a result of the instructions received from the Lord. It's from the Spirit and it begins to operate in the realm of the body. Faithfulness is not faith. See faith is a substance in Heb. 11:1 the substance of things hoped for the evidence of things not seen. But faithfulness is a character of having faith. And it means that your physical being and your whole body is now geared to obeying God continually.

When we say someone is faithful, we are also saying that person in times of difficulty has kept doing his job. When we say someone is faithful, we are saying in season or out of season, that person keeps on doing that job. In cold and in heat, in popularity and in persecution that person keeps doing the job - that is faithfulness. It talks about the deeds of the body and discipline. For you to have the full joy of the Lord, master faithfulness among the other parts of the fruit of the Spirit and enjoy life.

CHAPTER EIGHT

Joy and Gentleness

Gentleness is translated "meekness" in the King James Version. However, it is translated "gentleness" in most of the newer English versions. This is not a matter of any difference in the ancient Greek manuscripts of the New Testament. The Greek word **prautes** is found in them all. The problem here is that the English language has changed since the days of King James and Shakespeare. The common dictionary definition of meekness as it is used today is "deficient in spirit and courage." That is a far cry from the meaning of the Greek word. Gentleness is when you care enough to choose not to be harsh, rash, angry, or rough. Gentleness is when you know and use the best way to hold an egg or a butterfly. A gentle person knows better than to harm others, and so chooses to act in a way that does not.

The word gentleness means meekness, mild mannered or meek. That is the eighth step. Now meekness has come upon your life. Now when God's Spirit leads you, you know you are right. You don't have to justify yourself. To be meek is to let God justify you. You don't even have to prove that you are right. If you are right you are right – there is no need to prove it and God will back you up. The book of Numbers tells us how when Moses was challenged by Aaron and Miriam, he was described as the meekest.

Gentleness In Our Lives

Meekness means that even though that something could be done in the flesh you refuse to go in the flesh but you rather let God's Spirit bring it forth. Meekness is a quality that David had when two times he had the opportunity to kill Saul. At first he almost did. He cut off a piece of Saul's garment and his heart smote him. The bible did not say the Lord smote him but it says his heart smote him

I remember a certain gentleman who used to come to our ministry and this same man had a big problem with infidelity that his wife did not know at the time. At one time he was even caught red handed. You see this guy had gone around accusing us of all sorts. He slandered my husband and even his wife joined in. One day the husband was caught red handed by two people in the church and he confessed. This was something that we could have used to attack him for all the lies he spread about us BUT gentleness chooses not to do such a thing. We had a chance to do something to hurt this man and his wife with the information we had but meekness did not allow us. We had obtained a chance to use this information to prove our case but we did not. Joy was in us and until today, we have kept it and will continue to keep the name of this person private.

You see this man had set himself up for destruction when he started going around accusing gentle people. Gentleness means that something could be done in the flesh but you refuse to go in the flesh you'd rather let God's Spirit bring it forth. We could have sprung into action and nailed that guy but we have too much joy coming out of these parts of the fruit that it is all good to shut our mouths.

A gentle person does not seek to make other people suffer. Gentleness may seem to lose battles, but it helps win the overall struggles. A gentle response tends to create fewer enemies, and more friends. However Gentleness can also be bold. Webster's Dictionary does give an older meaning for meekness as "enduring injury with patience and without resentment." That might not be too far from the meaning of the biblical word, but the Greek is much more positive. Gentleness is never self-important but is considerate, courteous, and modest, yet willing to try when a job needs to be done.

Like the other parts of the spiritual fruit, gentleness is an aspect of God's character which

God's followers take on as they follow Christ. They receive it when they follow Christ but they need to practise it in order to get joy in its fullness. As you have seen, 'gentleness' isn't about being weak but a refusal to use power to harm anyone when you know you can. Gentleness is an unwillingness to wound them for vengeance's sake. Gentleness is about the power to subdue the power to harm. It is a gentle way to be bold, to be non-violent but still have power to stand up for what is right, and non-manipulative ways to lead.

However it is not human nature to be gentle. We are simply not gentle creatures but when Christ comes gentleness is imparted in our spirits but the soul still needs to be saved in order for gentleness to be practiced. Today's world gives rewards to hostility and going to an extreme. If we are to bear the fruit of gentleness, we need the Spirit to give us the ability to practice gentleness when it's hardest to be that way. We need to practice gentleness regardless of the fire circumstance bring our way.

There Is Power In Gentleness

Do you see that all the parts of the fruit of the spirit contain power instead of weakness? Notice love itself which is the fruit or the ultimate sum total of all these parts as indicated in chapter one. The Lord Jesus Christ says love your enemies and it will be like pouring hot coals of fire on them.

Do you see that? When one uses the sum total that promotes joy and includes joy itself they become sizzling hot to all their problems including their enemies. It might look like this is not the case because all these parts look very passive when they are really not. In fact one of the reasons why they look like they are very passive is because we have been taught wrongly.

You see Gentleness has power in it. Notice to understand gentleness further, let us go through the passages in the Bible where the Greek word prautes is used. In the Old Testament the Septuagint uses it once in Psalm 45:4. The Psalmist calls on God;

"Gird thy sword upon thy thigh, O most Mighty, with thy glory and thy majesty. And in thy majesty ride prosperously, because of truth and gentleness and righteousness" (Psalm 45:3,4).

Gentleness is not weakness. It is not allowing yourself to become a doormat. It is part of God's character as He moves gloriously in mighty power and victory. It takes courage to be gentle in the midst of all the evil surrounding us in this world.

Be Gentle In Your Words

Gentleness is not measured by what you do only but also on what you say and how you respond to situations in life. How you answer others is also a measurement of how gentle you are.

Look at Proverbs 15:1

"...A soft answer turneth away wrath: but grievous words stir up anger..."

A soft word turns aside bad feelings, strife and discord. But words that are harsh just stir things up. A good proverb for us to know.

Following a very successful conference in the Caribbean Island one time, a radio DJ was out to discredit the numerous miracles that had taken place. This guy was an atheist, (if there is such a thing as an atheist), who made it his duty to try and discredit what he had heard. With a negative spin, he invited the listeners to phone in and discuss. He did not expect what took place when he opened the phone lines. He was shocked when every call became a testimonial. I should stress that all the phone calls that came in that day were from people who had been healed of one disease or the other. Many of them even offered to take the guy to their doctors to confirm their miracles.

When he saw that everyone was testifying to the healings and the prophecies, he started saying things about preachers only wanting money. That was until one person, herself a journalist and leader of one of the churches that were present at the conference, called him and informed him that we had given the churches thousands of dollars and had come to the Caribbean Islands at our own expense. We did not take any money. In fact we had sown back into the churches that arranged the conference.

You see at that time we could have called in

ourselves and given him a piece of each of our minds my husband and I. We could also have sent the team we had travelled with to call and shout but we didn't. We knew the guy was an atheist but we did not explore it. Gentleness in our deeds caused all his accusations to fall on deaf ears.

And you know what I've learned? Being harsh towards someone else never solves a problem. It just brings about bad feelings. It postpones your problems. You've seen this for yourself. You've been in many situations where something happened where you felt that the proper response included 'breaking someone down'. The proper response then was to kill someone or do some harm. I know right now as you read this you have few people that you thought could be helped by a little beating. However gentleness calls for a stronger power to subdue those feelings especially when you possess the power to harm or revenge.

Be Gentle In Life

It should be repeated that gentleness is when you care enough to choose not to be harsh, angry, or rough when you have the chance to do it. Gentleness is when you know and use the best way to hold an egg or a butterfly. A gentle person knows better than to harm others, and so chooses to act in a way that does not harm them and even goes to the extent of helping that person. A gentle person does not seek to make other people angry. Gentleness may lose battles, but it helps win the overall struggles. A gentle response tends to create fewer enemies, and more friends. Gentleness is a sweetness of character and softness of manners. This has often been attributed as a feminine characteristic that men should never show but is this explanation given in the Bible?

2 Timothy 2:24-26 says;

"And the Lord's servant must not be quarrelsome but kind to everyone, able to teach, patiently enduring evil, correcting his opponents with gentleness. God may perhaps grant them repentance leading to a knowledge of the truth, and they may escape from the snare of the devil, after being captured by him to do his will."

This is something that all followers of Christ are called to do.

Titus 3:1-2 addresses this same issue;

"Remind them to be submissive to rulers and authorities, to be obedient, to be ready for every good work, to speak evil of no one, to avoid quarrelling, to be gentle, and to show perfect courtesy toward all people."

Who can say that they have mastered gentleness? We continually need the Lord's help to show courtesy and avoid quarrels so we need the word everyday to enter our hearts so we can be impregnated by an ability to be gentle. Gentleness is not a trait that is often valued in our society. Power to harm makes other nations superpowers. Fierceness seems to gain people more respect. However we are shown, over and over, in the word of God, that gentleness is a sign of a mature Christian. Knowing Jesus Christ and walking with the Spirit gives us the great power of Christ.

Do you see now that at a deeper level gentleness is power under control? It is power to control the power one has. It is the ability to be like God. Though he knows we should die because of the sins we commit he restrains from using that power to destroy humanity. All this is because of gentleness.

Psalms 18:35 shows us that God is our example and support in gentleness.

"You have given me the shield of your salvation and your right hand supported me and your gentleness made me great"

Think of Moses. He was the meekest of all men as written in the word, and yet he confronted Pharaoh, led the Israelites through the wilderness, dealt with their unbelief and complaints, and had a close relationship with God.

The Lord Jesus said in Matthew 11 vs. 28-30;

"Come to Me, all you who labor and are heavy laden, and I will give you rest. Take My yoke upon you and learn from Me, for I am gentle and lowly in heart..."

Jesus spoke of being gentle, or meek, and lowly in heart, or humble and immediately He says He can carry the heaviest of yokes, yours and mine. Do you see the ability and power gentleness carries?

Gentleness also means having a teachable spirit where one can be taught and learn something from people or things regardless of how knowledgeable they are. You see there are some people who know nothing but who have convinced themselves that they know a lot. I meet a lot of these people in business and also in the house of God. They like to teach others but cannot spare a minute to learn. My husband can sit down and listen to people that take him as a spiritual father. His mind is renewed to know that God can speak to these people too so he decided to practice meekness. He is not puffed up because of the achievements God has given him. You see when a person has no gentleness they cannot be taught anything. In their minds they know everything but even the Master Teacher Jesus Christ Himself was teachable, not puffed up with His own perfection.

Christians are to develop this admirable part of the fruit of the Spirit and retain this quality at all times. Self-importance has no place in the Body of Christ. Notice what the Bible says in Gal 6 vs. 1

"Brethren, if a man is overtaken in any trespass, you who are spiritual restore such a one in a spirit of gentleness, considering yourself lest you also be tempted."

Gentleness should cause a person to understand that others who are persecuting them have not reached the same spiritual level like they have done. In that understanding should come out a way of understanding them that will cause you to be gentle when they persecute you and gossip about you.

How To Develop Gentleness

Gentleness comes from a deep walk with the word of God. The word when you meditate on it causes you to be very submissive. It removes all harshness and anger and causes you to be a winner in life. Gentleness does not come through wearing long dresses, jezebel had that. It's not in being around men of God; Judas had the ultimate man around him. Gentleness is in the word and practicing it and not just being around men of God. Look at what Peter said;

1 Peter 3:3-4

Your beauty should not come from outward adornment, such as braided and the wearing of gold jewellery and fine clothes. Instead, it should be that of your inner self, the unfading beauty of a gentle and quiet spirit, which is of great worth in God's sight. (NIV)

With the cultivation of self control also comes gentleness. Gentleness needs the hand of your spirit to get a hold of your flesh so that you become a person of full joy. It is possible, and so can be done. One should also be able to control their own soul and spirit using all the parts of the fruit so as to be great people filled with joy everlasting and full of life.

This is a life of a mastering life.

CHAPTER NINE

Have Temperance

First we should notice what Proverbs 23 vs.2 says;

"...If you are a man given to appetite cut your throat..."

The above scripture is a great reflection of what temperance or self control is. It is your ability to rob the flesh and enrich your spirit. You see your flesh has the ability to accumulate things the Lord does not want you to have or own. The spirit then has to be strong enough through the first group of the fruit of the spirit to grab the flesh and rob it of what it wants to keep. This might sound very difficult to understand but for joy to be full there is need to really get the meaning of it.

The Greek word used in Galatians 5:23 is egkrateia, which means having command or mastery over, or possession of, one's own behaviour. In older

English, it was often translated as 'temperance', which was more about moderation than control.

According to the word of God you need to put a knife to your throat if you are given to appetite.

2 Peter 1 vs. 6 says of temperance add;

"...to knowledge TEMPERANCE..."

The word temperance is ENKRATEIA in Greek. This means 'to hold yourself from within'.

Man is spirit, possesses a soul and lives in a body but many times the body rules the man. The spirit should be the boss, the soul should be the supervisor and the body should be the worker.

However, for temperance or ENKRATEIA to happen, there is need to let the spirit be the boss like God made it. The only way to do it is to suppress the body like Apostle Paul said:

"I bring my body under..."

Your body has many requests that are contrary to the spirit and would want those requests met no matter the day or time. If you manage to be temperate (enkrateia) you will win the battle and be able to control your life.

ENKRATEIA yourself: hold yourself from within. Don't do a lot of things that are not necessary. For example, people spend more than they bring in, that means getting into serious debt. The debt worsens as they spend even more and they end up in debt crisis. The same goes for people with addictions. Instead of stopping they fall deeper and deeper until stopping seems impossibility. Self control is crucial not only to live in the full joy of the Lord but for basic spiritual growth.

Pushing Yourself Beyond Your Ability

That is the same in life. Remember the word says in the book of Romans 12 vs. 3;

"...be it prophecy let it be done according to the measure of faith"

Don't try to push out what you have not deposited. You see there is a tendency to try and push ourselves where our faith cannot take us. This is also lack of temperance. This is lack of self control. I remember when my husband went to a certain church in Africa to preach for a certain minister. In that church where he was preaching there were many preachers who loved the office that he is used in as a prophet. There were certain preachers though who desired to move in the same office at any cost without being sent by God. We saw serious mistakes in the prophetic that eventually affected the people all because of lack of self control.

They could not run their own race. They wanted to reproduce the gift and in their reproducing they made a lot of mistakes. Self control was not practised. They went beyond where their faith could take them. They went by their flesh and suppressed the spirit that it could not overtake the flesh in its need to copy. You see zeal is fine if it is in the Lord but when one is not in agreement with God it becomes bad.

Those understood their call are being used even more in their office for honouring what my husband had received from God without a need to mimic anything. Do you see this example?

People need to get to a level where they stay in their own race and not try to run other people's races. My husband and I have decided to stay where we were called to be regardless of what people say or what circumstances bring. We have self control. We have enkrateia!

Self control in finances and in life

I gave an example earlier about self control when it comes to spending. This is a very important principle when it comes to your finances. You need to take control of your spending. Cut back on luxuries until such time when the wealth of the wicked is now in your grasp. Appetites should be reduced. If you like extra special designer clothes, wail until a time when shops have a sale or something and buy your yearly clothes. Just after Christmas in most countries January and February are months reserved for good bargains. This is the time to buy clothes for all seasons. Don't buy things that you simply cannot afford because you cannot control yourself. The Lord said "if your eye causes you to sin pluck it out", and His word also says in Proverbs 23 vs. 2;

"If you are a person given to appetite put a knife to your throat"

When the scripture says put a knife to your throat, it does not mean to literally commit suicide. No it doesn't. It simply means you need to limit your appetite for things. Take control of your spending. Limit your spending. Spend only when it is necessary. There will come a time when you go into a shop without a thought of whether or not your card has enough credit on it.

I have met hundreds of people who are simply not happy because they are in deep financial problems. Their joy has been stolen by the enemy and they simply cannot muster strength to get their joy back again. As I mentioned before, if you need to get out of debt there is a need for you to control your spending. This does not necessarily mean you no longer get the same things you used to have. All it means is you might need to spend less on the same things.

Hold yourself from within. Hold your body by the hand of the spirit. ENKRATEIA yourself!

For Joy To Work

As aforementioned, what makes this revelation of superior power to other subjects devoted to joy is that this is God given and also that this covers the whole person, spirit, soul and body. At the same time the components of love as the fruit of the Spirit are also in groups by themselves. For joy to work in your life, always remember the parts of the fruit of the Spirit and how to apply them. Your joy will not be full if you do not do so.

A Summary Of The Parts Of The Fruit Of The Spirit And The Interlink

Joy: Different to happiness, only happiness requires right circumstances where joy does not. Jesus Christ felt joy though He faced heavy trials (Hebrews 12:2). We should all be joyful having been called by God.

Peace: Peace of mind and peace with God. This is a force that can crush your enemies because when one has peace with God they can have peace with anyone even those who try to harm them. (Philippians 4:6-7).

Longsuffering: Allowing your fire to keep on burning. Focussing on adding fire to an extent where it cannot be quenched by anything thrown at you. It also involves bearing with others who are working out their salvation. Being slow to anger (Romans 15:1; Luke 21:19).

Kindness: This part of the fruit is also a force. It is not passive though it looks passive. Behaving toward others kindly, as God has behaved toward us (Ephesians 4:31-32).

Goodness: Generosity of spirit that springs from imitating Jesus Christ (Psalm 33:4-5). Just being a good person.

Faithfulness: Being reliable. Respect the time of the command. This describes a person who is trustworthy and will always stand up for God's way. We can count on, and should work at imitating, the faithfulness of God (Philippians 1:6; Hebrews 13:5).

Gentleness: Considerate and tactful in conduct and correction. Never get angry at the wrong time. (Matthew 5:22-24; Ephesians 4:26).

Self-Control: Discipline which gives us victory over the wrong pulls of our mind and body.

(I John 2:15-17).

These groups are in connection with the spirit, soul and body. This fruit controls your spirit, controls your soul and controls your body. As we have already seen, we are spirit beings, who possess a soul and live in a body. If you look again at Galatians 5:22-23, you will notice that the first two parts of love as the fruit of the Spirit **joy** and **peace** are always the basic control of our spirit man. If your spirit man is right with God, you will have these. **Longsuffering, kindness and goodness** have everything to do with controlling your soul. Your soul consists of mind, will and emotions, so longsuffering, kindness and goodness control your mind, will and emotions. They control your soul.

The last three **faithfulness, gentleness and self-control** speak of control of **your body** and master it into submission to the will of the Spirit and in turn, the control of all these three areas by the Spirit bring full joy.

These parts make up the fruit of the Spirit which is love. Without love you cannot get these principles to work, it is impossible for love is the sum total of all these parts. Love is the fruit of the Spirit and the products of that love are the ones we have dealt with in this book.

These principles will have your spirit, your soul and your body subordinate to the spiritual influences of the Holy Spirit and you will have great joy. Kick back, cool down, relax and by the leading of the Holy Spirit, I challenge you from this point onwards – to ENJOY LIFE NOW!